MISOGYNIES

Joan Smith was born in London in 1953. She was educated at Reading University and then trained as a journalist on the *Evening Gazette* in Blackpool. She joined the *Sunday Times* in 1979, first as a member of the Insight team, and then as a general reporter. She has been a free-lance writer and journalist since 1984, and has established a considerable reputation as a writer of crime fiction with *A Masculine Ending* (tele-vised by the BBC in April 1992), *Why Aren't They Screaming* and *Don't Leave Me This Way*. *Misogynies* was first published in 1989 to excep-tional critical acclaim.

# MISOGYNIES

## Reflections on Myths and Malice

## JOAN SMITH

*faber and faber*

LONDON · BOSTON

for Gill Williams

First published in 1989
by Faber and Faber Limited
3 Queen Square London WC1N 3AU
Paperback edition first published in 1990
This revised paperback edition first published in 1993

Printed in England by Clays Ltd, St Ives plc

© Joan Smith, 1989

'Immaculate Misconceptions' first appeared in shorter form as
'Mary, Mary, quite uncontrary' in the *New Statesman*; 'Crawling
From the Wreckage' first appeared in shorter form in *New
Statesman and Society* as 'Ghost Flyers in the Sky'.

A CIP record for this book is
available from the British Library

ISBN 0–571–16807–8

2 4 6 8 10 9 7 5 3 1

# CONTENTS

Is it not really remarkable (we ask ourselves in amazement), when one considers the overwhelming mass of this transparent material, that so little recognition and attention are paid to the fact of men's secret dread of women?

Karen Horney, *The Dread of Women*, 1932

Women have very little idea of how much men hate them.

Germaine Greer, *The Female Eunuch*, 1970

It's then I think on't Ripper
an what e did an why,
an ow mi mates ate women,
an ow Pete med em die

Blake Morrison, 'The Ballad of
the Yorkshire Ripper', 1985

# PREFACE TO THE REVISED EDITION

When I began writing *Misogynies,* in late December 1987, I had little idea of how the book would be received. It was, in essence, a challenge to myself: a test of my theory that the same pernicious attitudes were at work in disparate and apparently unconnected aspects of Western culture. I finished the book with a sense of quiet satisfaction—it seemed to me that the case was proved—but I still did not know what would happen when it was exposed to an audience beyond the few close friends who had read it in progress.

*Misogynies* was published in Britain in 1989, and in the United States a couple of years later. Letters from readers began to arrive almost at once. They have never stopped. By now I have heard from women (and men) all over the world—from Britain, Germany, Australia, New Zealand, South Africa, Brazil, Canada, and from many parts of the United States. Out of all these hundreds of letters, only a handful have been hostile; *Misogynies* seems to have struck a chord with a wide cross section of readers.

One of the questions I am most frequently asked about the book concerns what *isn't* in it; why no chapter on pop music, say, or surrealist painting or men's clubs like Bohemian Grove? One reader suggested, only partly in jest, that I should update the book with quarterly bulletins. Yet *Misogynies* was never intended to be comprehensive. It states its case and provides a method, one which the reader can apply to a whole range of subjects the book doesn't attempt to cover. I have, nevertheless, written two additional chapters for this new edition, each of them a response to events that have taken place since the book was finished. The collapse of autocratic Communist rule in Eastern Europe prompted me to examine my uneasiness about the attitude to women of a dissident writer who has achieved almost iconic status in the West; the result is an analysis of the work of Milan Kundera which I have called 'Czech Mate'. Shortly before this new edition went to press, America was convulsed by the controversy over the nomination of Judge Clarence Thomas to the Supreme Court and Professor Anita Hill's accusation that he had sexually harassed her. My reflections on the episode, which is a classic example of the covert operation of misogyny, open the book in a chapter entitled 'Doubting Thomas'.

'Hope for the best, expect the worst', advises a character in Angela Carter's novel *Wise Children*. I count myself fortunate that the critical and popular response to *Misogynies* has exceeded my wildest expectations; this new edition rounds out and completes the project I began in 1987. I take this opportunity to thank my readers, whose enthusiasm has confirmed my belief both in the power of ideas and in the new confidence of women which is a prerequisite for change.

*Joan Smith*
*Kidlington, Oxford*
*January 1992*

# INTRODUCTION

If this book has a single starting-point, it is the case of the multiple murderer Peter Sutcliffe, universally known as the Yorkshire Ripper. Ten years ago, in 1978, I arrived at a radio station in Manchester as an enthusiastic but inexperienced journalist. I was twenty-five, keen to get on, and new to the city. I expected life to be packed with exciting news stories, which it was, and one of them happened to be the continuing saga of the Yorkshire Ripper. By that time he was thought to have killed ten women, two of them—in spite of the nickname—in Manchester. A few months later, in April 1979, Josephine Whitaker, a building society clerk, was savagely murdered in Halifax. I was sent to a police press conference where I interviewed George Oldfield, head of the band of West Yorkshire detectives known as the Ripper Squad, and was dismayed by his masculine bluster and the unhealthy scarlet that suffused his round face. As yet, my lack of confidence in him was unformed, built on little more than a fleeting impression, and I was more deeply affected by the nightmare horror of the case: eleven women dead in a manner which had not been revealed but was rumoured to involve terrible mutilations; several others alive but haunted by memories of their terrible ordeal at the hands of the killer. Like other women working at the radio station, I was constantly aware of my dual role of reporter and potential victim; by day I reported the latest developments in the story, by night I could not sleep when I

returned to the Manchester suburb where I lived alone. One of
the early victims had died in her own home, and my professional
status was no protection; I already doubted the police's strongly
held conviction that the murderer's prime target was prostitutes.
Why I felt this I cannot really say, other than that it seemed too
glib, too 'psychological' an explanation. What I was struck by,
I suppose, was the fact that these were crimes directed against
*women*. I must already have been half-aware of the theories
outlined in this book, and it seemed to me that the crimes
expressed a simple, virulent loathing of the female which did not
need fancy explanations like those arrived at by the police.

When Barbara Leach, a student at Bradford University, became the next victim in September 1979, I was close to despair.
In this I was not alone. I vividly remember the faces of the other
women in the newsroom when we heard that another Ripper
murder had taken place, their faces wiped of all expression except
the sudden blankness of shock and fear. I did not believe that the
detectives of the Ripper Squad were capable of catching the
killer, and in this I was proved right. When Peter Sutcliffe finally
appeared at the Old Bailey in 1981, he owed his arrest to two
South Yorkshire policemen who had spotted the false number
plates on his car while they were on a routine patrol. That the
Yorkshire Ripper was finally behind bars was an immense relief,
even though I was no longer living in the north of England, but
the interpretation of the case at which I had gradually arrived
offered me little comfort. For many years I had assumed that I
was living in a society that was unfair to women, an environment
that was sometimes hostile to them, but that this was no more
than a hangover from history, an unthinking allegiance to an
outdated way of organizing everyday affairs. Now that women,
especially feminist women in Britain and the United States, were
challenging the old assumptions, standing up for their rights, it

would not be long before people recognized the disadvantages under which they laboured and things changed for the better. Peter Sutcliffe made me realize that I was wrong; that only a culture which nurtured and encouraged a deep-seated hatred of women could produce a mass killer of his type, and that when it did, it was hardly to be wondered at that its agents were unable to distinguish him from the mass of its products. The discrimination and denigration and violence that women suffer are no historical accident but linked manifestations of this hatred; I inhabit a culture which is not simply sexist but *occasionally lethal* for women. Misogyny wears many guises, reveals itself in different forms which are dictated by class, wealth, education, race, religion, and other factors, but its chief characteristic is its pervasiveness. So powerful is it that society is organized along lines which sanction the separation of the sexes to an extraordinary degree. Nor is woman-hating found only in the male half of the human race. We are all exposed to the prevailing ideology of our culture, and some women learn early that they can prosper by aping the misogyny of men; these are the women who win provisional favour by denigrating other women, by playing on male prejudices, and by acting the 'man's woman'. The rest of us get by as best we can, often denying what we know because it is painful to admit that we live in circumstances which not only restrict our freedom but physically threaten us if we step out of line: in this culture, the penalty for being a woman is sometimes death.

The excuse, the only justification for this shocking state of affairs, comes from those who claim that, flawed though it is, unfortunate as are some of its consequences, the present organizational structure of society has a 'natural', biological basis. To accept this notion of inescapable difference between men and women denies us both a discussion of its consequences and of the possibility of change. Therefore the question I would put to proponents of the anatomy-is-destiny theory is this: are you *happy* with this state of affairs? Can you shrug off the fact that women are routinely denigrated, despised, segregated, raped, mutilated and murdered? Are you saying, in fact, that it is *natural* for men to hate and fear women?

I do not believe that this is the case, and I remain unimpressed by the arguments of anatomy-is-destiny theorists. For that reason I can allow myself to hope; without hope, faint as it is, I could not have written this book. I have called it *Misogynies*, both because the manifestations of the phenomenon I have addressed take so many forms, and because I owe the book's structure to another and more eloquent piece of social analysis, *Mythologies* by Roland Barthes. Writing it has been a difficult, frequently painful and occasionally uplifting experience, in which I have benefited enormously from discussions with and support from many people. The theory and analysis in the book are mine alone, as are its faults, but it could not have been written without Carol Baker, Anthony Barnett, Anita Bennett, Frances Coady, Judith Herrin, Ian Irvine, Judy Jackson, Linda Lewis, Imogen Parker, Jane Shilling and Stuart Weir (in all of whom I have thus far failed to detect evidence of the morbid attitudes about which I have been writing). Francis Wheen provided, as ever, living proof of the possibility of a philogynous future. To Rosemary Goad I owe a special debt of thanks, one which I here acknowledge with heartfelt gratitude.

*Steeple Aston,*
*May 1988*

# MISOGYNIES

# DOUBTING THOMAS

In October 1991 the House of Lords removed a centuries-old right from the men of England and Wales: it stopped them raping their wives.

I exaggerate, of course. Even the highest court in the land cannot prevent husbands from forcing their wives to have sex against their will, but it did remove the immunity from prosecution they had enjoyed since 1736. In that year a ruling by a seventeenth-century judge, Sir Matthew Hale, was published and accepted as a definitive statement of law; according to Hale, a woman agreed to sex when she married and could never, ever change her mind. He said:

> A husband cannot be guilty of a rape committed by himself upon his lawful wife, for by their mutual matrimonial consent and contract the wife hath given herself up in this kind unto her husband which she cannot retract.

Even the English law lords, all male and by no means radical, found this hard to stomach in 1991. Upholding the conviction of a 38-year-old man jailed for assaulting and attempting to rape his estranged wife, they agreed that Hale's ruling was an 'anachronistic and offensive' fiction. Yet their opinion, sensible as it may seem, did not meet with universal approval. Neil Lyndon, the biographer of Armand Hammer, denounced the ruling in the *Spectator* as a victory for a 'totalitarian group' motivated by a 'terror of Eros'. The law lords, according to Lyndon, were the dupes of a 'feminist orthodoxy' which 'insists that male sexuality is actively antagonistic to women':

> When their Lordships shifted the law on rape in marriage, they acceded to and gave established respectability to the idea that normal men are rapists. We may wish that they endure many hours of brow-beating perplexity in conducting this principle through the courts.[1]

The interesting thing about Lyndon's claim is its illogicality: the long campaign for a change in the law on rape in marriage rested on the assumption that there *is* a difference between rape and consensual sex, and that most people understand it. A few paragraphs later Lyndon moved on to another case turning on sexual *mores,* that of the United States Senate hearings into the nomination of Judge Clarence Thomas to the Supreme Court, which he construed as a partial victory for phallophobic feminists.

The hearings, according to Lyndon, 'revealed another measure of the extent to which the intolerant attitudes of the sisterhood have penetrated the life of the West, not so much in the evidence which was given as in the commentaries upon the case'. Specifically:

> Editors and columnists everywhere thundered the news that men must adjust their moral bearing to the new realities of professional and commercial life, in which women as equal colleagues had a right to pursue their work without unseemly leerings from the water-cooler

and indecent boasting about the pleasures they were missing. These admonitions seem to be inherently decent and
incontestable; but they do not take account of the deeply
altered state of affairs at work for men and women: they
do not allow for the truth that all places of work which
include men and women in roughly equal numbers are
hectic cockpits of sexual interest, flirtation, intrigue and
scheming, in which women are just as likely as men to
make advances and, if they are spurned, to be spiteful in
revenge.

For Lyndon, the presence of women in the workplace transforms it from a neutral into a sexual space. No longer a refuge
from women—apart from those safely clustered at the bottom of
the hierarchy—the office is reconstituted as a stage for sexual
games in which women participate as enthusiastically as men.
Some women welcome this notion of themselves as predators in
a sexual contest; the Irish writer Mary Kenny, commenting on
the Thomas hearings in the ultraconservative *Sunday Telegraph,*
bemoaned the fact that she had not been sexually harassed at work
and commended women who use their 'sex appeal' to 'get on in
life':

> . . . plenty of women like being seductive and exercising
> powers of sexuality over men. It's fun. It's amusing seeing
> otherwise purposeful men being reduced to the supplicat-
> ing male; just watch a skilfully seductive woman turn the
> sex game into cat-and-mouse play; she, of course, being
> the feline.[2]

There is a cavalier, all's-fair-in-love-and-war attitude here
that misses an important point: it assumes that men and women

are equal, willing players in any 'sex game' that goes on at work. Women who complain, by this token, are bad losers—which is precisely the charge laid against Clarence Thomas's accuser, Professor Anita Hill, by his second wife, Virginia Lamp Thomas. She told *People* magazine:

> ... what's scary about her allegations is that they remind me of the movie *Fatal Attraction* or, in her case, what I call the fatal assistant. In my heart, I always believed she was probably someone in love with my husband and never got what she wanted.[3]

Or, in the words of the young black man overheard in a Harlem restaurant by writer and editor Rosemary L. Bray, 'Clarence got jungle fever, and [Anita Hill] got mad'.[4] Judging by opinion polls, the notion of Professor Hill as a woman scorned, weaving malicious fantasies to get revenge, seems to have appealed to a majority of Americans; a poll carried out for the *New York Times*[5] and CBS News shortly after she gave evidence suggested that 58 percent were sceptical of her claim that Judge Thomas had pestered her for dates, boasted of his sexual prowess and described the content of pornographic films. Less than a quarter of those polled—24 percent—thought she was the more credible witness. Yet it is hard to imagine a worse forum than the Senate Judiciary Committee for eliciting the truth of Anita Hill's allegations. Members of the committee who questioned Hill and Thomas during lengthy, televised proceedings were out to prove preexisting opinions formed largely on party lines—which produced, among other incongruities, the comic spectacle of Senator Ted Kennedy in the role of feminist champion. 'It would not be easy', wrote Nicholas von Hoffman, 'to find 14 other men in America less suited by birth, wealth and life experience to fathom the motives of an Anita Hill'.[6] Faced with two professional people, each of them a credible, compelling witness, how was the Judiciary Committee—and the vast majority of senators who weren't even on it—to come to a decision?

The figures show that most senators simply made up their minds on party lines. All but two of the 43 Republicans voted for the nomination, and 46 Democrats against. Eleven Democrats voted yes, seven of them from Southern states where they depend on the black vote for survival. In that sense, the confirmation of Judge Thomas by a majority of only two was neither a declaration of his innocence nor a crushing blow to Professor Hill's credibility. What it did do was split the black community, infuriate women's groups, and encumber the Supreme Court with a lame duck nominee for anything up to the next four decades.

It also, and this is the only positive outcome of the case, stimulated a fierce debate about sexual conduct at work on both sides of the Atlantic. Newspapers commissioned polls which appeared to show a startlingly high incidence of sexual harassment in offices, shops and factories—the *Independent on Sunday* suggested immediately after the hearings that 'nearly two million working women'[7] in Britain had been victims. The same paper reported that the problem was now taken seriously by 'a clear majority of both men and women,' and that there was broad agreement on what kind of behaviour constituted harassment. In that sense, it is hardly surprising if male sexual supremacists like Neil Lyndon are starting to panic, for they are right in thinking they have all but lost the argument. The sympathetic stance of a wide range of commentators on sexual harassment, and the law lords' ruling on marital rape, are symptoms of the same trend—of women successfully challenging rules of sexual conduct in the home and at work in whose making they had little or no say.

Yet now we arrive at a paradox. One woman, Professor

Anita Hill, is widely credited with bringing the subject of sexual harassment out into the open. A majority of people now seem to accept its existence and the need to do something about it. At the same time, a majority of Americans, at least, appear to think Anita Hill was lying.

The obvious conclusion, if you had been living on Mars in October 1991 and missed the Senate hearings, would be that Professor Hill's case against Judge Thomas was riddled with obvious lies and inconsistences. Yet the *New York Times* reported that one legal expert—Michael Schatzow, a Baltimore criminal defence lawyer and a former Federal prosecutor—had 'said that in legal terms, Professor Hill had a jury-swaying aura of credibility and the weight of much of the evidence in her favor'.[8] That evidence included the testimony of four friends, including another law professor and a woman judge, who said they had known about Judge Thomas's alleged behaviour long before Professor Hill agreed, reluctantly and under pressure from Democratic senators on the Judiciary Committee, to make it public. Professor Hill passed a lie detector test administered by a polygraph expert who used to work for the FBI, and an impressive number of journalists, commenting on her demeanour as a witness, described her testimony in phrases like 'devastatingly credible'. Two other former employees of Judge Thomas came forward to say that he had made sexual remarks to them while he was their boss at the Equal Employment Opportunity Commission in 1984 and 1985.

What about the case *against* Anita Hill? The notion that she was politically motivated did not survive the revelation of her own conservative politics, including her support for the right-wing Supreme Court nominee, Robert Bork, in 1987. Her failure to make an official complaint about Thomas at the time of the alleged harassment drew a sympathetic reaction from thousands of women who have remained silent in similar circumstances; when I was grabbed and kissed by a dee-jay at the radio station where I worked in 1979, I struggled free but did not complain to the management because he was a far more valued employee than I was. Nor was I suffering from divided loyalties; Anita Hill's dilemma, as a young black woman thinking of bringing damaging charges against a black man she admired, hardly seems to have been considered. Senator Orrin Hatch, a fanatical Mormon from Utah, suggested that Professor Hill's evidence was invented for the curious reason that the abuse she catalogued was not sufficiently original; Judge Thomas's alleged remarks about a character called 'Long Dong Silver', and about pubic hair on his Coke, had been featured, he said, in a previous sexual harassment case and in the novel *The Exorcist*. By this token, the incidents in an office where I worked in the early 1980s, when a fellow-employee used to sidle up and fantasise about joining the 'eight-mile-high club' by having sex with me in an airplane toilet, also did not take place.

But what seems to have carried the most weight against Professor Hill is not the evidence—which, in my view, tends to bear out her version of events rather than Judge Thomas's—but the vehemence of his denials. The vehemence *and* the content: there was open shock, an audible indrawing of breath, when Thomas chose to stake his defence on America's guilt for its long history of mistreatment of black men. In a furious and powerful speech, he rounded on his accusers and accused them of being a latter-day lynch mob:

> This is a circus, it's a national disgrace and from my
> standpoint as a black American . . . it's a high-tech

lynching for uppity blacks. It is a message that . . . you
will be lynched, destroyed, caricatured by a committee
of the US Senate rather than hung from a tree.[9]

Thomas's charge, that he was being judged not by his peers
but by members of a race which had persecuted his forefathers,
had obvious force; it was even more true of Anita Hill, who was
an outsider in the committee room on grounds of race *and*
gender. Yet Judge Thomas's clever and emotive use of the race
card had a devastating effect on Professor Hill's role in the
proceedings: as a black woman accusing a black man of sexual
misconduct, she had no place in his scenario at all. The classic
target of the lynch mob was—as, notoriously, in *Gone With the
Wind*—the black man accused of violating a *white* woman. By
raising this spectre, Judge Thomas highlighted his own blackness
and effectively erased that of his accuser, so much so that Americans found themselves being told they must choose between the
rights of blacks and of women, as though the categories were
mutually exclusive. Rosemary L Bray, in an anguished commen-
tary on the case, showed an acute understanding of what had been
done to the professor. She wrote that Anita Hill:

> confronted and ultimately breached a series of taboos in
> the black community that have survived both slavery and
> the post-segregation life she and Clarence Thomas share.
> Anita Hill put her private business in the street, and she
> downgraded a black man to a room filled with white
> men who might alter his fate—surely a large enough
> betrayal for her to be read out of the race.[10]

Professor Hill was so effectively 'read out of the race' that
her punishment came in the traditional form meted out not to

'uppity blacks' but to 'uppity' women—her sanity was questioned and she was disbelieved. A revealing report in the *New York Times* suggested that where Judge Thomas's breaking of taboo—by speaking openly and emotionally about race—counted in his favour, Professor Hill's failure to live up to stereotyped expectations of female behaviour weighed against her:

> While the Oklahoma law professor was poised and likeable, these Senators confided, she seemed too controlled and unemotional to really tug at the heartstrings of the heartland, especially when compared with Judge Thomas's hot and emotional television appearances in which he cast himself as a martyr to the process and to racial discrimination. He was the one with tears in his eyes as he faced the Senate Judiciary Committee, after all, not she.
>
> Many Senators had also found Professor Hill an unsympathetic figure because, even if her story was true, she seemed too calculated and career-centred in staying with Clarence Thomas at the Education Department and the Equal Employment Opportunity Commission rather than 'storming out in a huff,' as one lobbyist explained it. Her career had not been hurt by Mr. Thomas, these Senators argued.[11]

There is a suggestion here that if only Professor Hill had been more feminine, less controlled, more senators would have believed her. Is this really credible? Plenty of people had already rushed to characterise her as a woman unbalanced by jealousy, as the vengeful Alex from *Fatal Attraction,* and it seems probable that the slightest display of emotion on her part would have played into their hands. The fact that two groups of observers could reach such conflicting conclusions about the same person—that she was a pushy, over-controlled career woman *and* a deranged fantasist bent on revenge—suggests that Anita Hill, far more than Clarence Thomas, was the victim of preconceptions, of stereotyping, of outdated notions about how a particular type of human being should behave.

Perhaps the lesson Anita Hill has taught us is that we haven't yet reached the stage when fine-sounding words about sexual harassment can be matched by actions—when a woman can get up in public, accuse her former boss of being a sex pest, talk dirty on TV (even if she is only repeating what someone else has said to her), *and* be believed. And maybe it also tells us something about the hierarchies of bigotry, about what happens when two sets of prejudices collide: *pace* Lennon and Ono, woman is not even the nigger of the world. Not yet, anyway.

1. *Spectator,* 23 November 1991
2. *Sunday Telegraph,* 20 October 1991
3. *People,* 11 November 1991
4. 'Taking Sides Against Ourselves,' *The New York Times Magazine,* 17 November 1991. 'Jungle fever,' according to Bray, is a code term, taken from the Spike Lee film of that name, for a black man's desire to sleep with a white woman—Judge Thomas's second wife, Virginia Lamp Thomas, is white. Bray's article is an eloquent account of the schism in the black community over the allegations against Judge Thomas and an impassioned defence of Professor Hill.
5. Reported in the *New York Times,* 15 October 1991
6. *Independent* magazine, 26 October 1991
7. *Independent on Sunday,* 20 October 1991
8. *New York Times,* 15 October 1991
9. *Newsweek,* 21 October 1991
10. 'Taking Sides Against Ourselves,' as quoted above.
11. *New York Times,* 16 October 1991

# M'LEARNED FRIENDS

Three or four times a year, we in Britain go through a ritual known as Outcry Over Judge's Remarks In Rape Case. What usually happens is that, faced with an offender who has terrified or beaten some poor woman into having sex against her will, a judge imposes a ludicrously light penalty with the observation that the victim's ordeal wasn't really so bad—or, indeed, that she should have known better than to get herself into the situation in the first place. Women's groups and MPs protest; in the very worst cases, the Lord Chancellor may even issue a rebuke. Then the whole business dies down—until it happens again.

Which makes the case of Edwin Fallen,[1] a twenty-seven-year-old would-be rapist who appeared at the Old Bailey in March 1988, all the more remarkable. Fallen went to a dance in Kilburn the previous November and met Karen Bell, twenty-two. The young woman had a drink with Fallen and went for a meal with him before inviting him back to her flat. There Fallen, who was apparently 'much encouraged' by the fact that she was wearing a short skirt, tried to have sex with her. When she pushed him away, he punched her in the face, breaking her jaw. He threatened to kill her unless she stopped screaming, and began pulling her clothes off. She was saved by the police who, called by her flatmate, found Fallen fondling her.

Fallen admitted indecent assault and causing grievous bodily harm. His counsel said the woman's behaviour at the dance had led him to believe he could have sexual intercourse with her. The judge, Mr Justice Rougier, then made an extraordinary statement. Women, he said, 'are entitled to dress attractively, even provocatively if you like, be friendly with casual acquaintances and still say no at the end of the evening without being brutally assaulted'. Gaoling Fallen for eighteen months, he added: 'This sort of brutal violence, particularly to women, has got to be dealt with severely. You broke her jaw just because she wasn't prepared to go to bed with you.'

Did Mr Justice Rougier know what he was doing? At a stroke, he had turned on its head the accumulated wisdom of years; he had abolished the unwritten code of behaviour against which a woman's behaviour has traditionally been measured before any complaint of rape or assault is allowed to stand. At long last, and certainly not before time, a judge had granted women, unconditionally, a liberty they had never before enjoyed: the freedom to say no. (His notion of a severe sentence might be open to challenge, but that is another matter.) He may not have realized it but, sitting up there in his wig and robes, Mr Justice Rougier had just articulated a new theory of sexual relations. A woman *can* dress as she likes; she *can* dance with a man, drink with him, even go back to her flat with him; and, at the end of the evening, she is still entitled to say no without fear of attack. She is entitled, in other words, to the freedoms that men have always taken for granted.

Just how significant a break with tradition is marked by the Fallen case can be established by a quick look at how the judiciary reacted in some other 1980s cases.

*Item*: In January 1988, only two months before Mr Justice Rougier made his remarks, a judge said that a twelve-year-old girl who had been raped had acted fool-ishly. Ian Kenworthy, nineteen, appeared before Lincoln High Court charged with raping the girl after she went back to his bed-sit for a cup of coffee. Sentencing him to three years' youth custody, Mr Justice John Evans said: 'It was foolish of her to go.' He also remarked: 'In other days, you would have said she was asking for trouble.'[2]

*Item*: In March 1986 a London magistrate suggested that any woman out late at night was likely to be a prostitute. Handing down a conditional discharge to a man accused of kerb crawling, he asked the police officer presenting the prosecution case: 'Are you trying to suggest that these women walking in that area at 1.25 A.M. could be there for any other reason than prostitution?' The incident happened near a busy tube station and in an area with an all-night bus service.[3]

*Item*: In December 1982 a man was acquitted of raping a thirty-one-year-old woman at a flat in Cambridge. The woman claimed she had been raped after meeting the man in a pub. The jury was told she submitted because she was afraid of being hurt. In his summing-up, Judge David Wild said: 'Women who say no do not always mean no. It is not just a question of saying no. It is a question of how she says it, how she shows and makes it clear. If she doesn't want it, she only has to keep her legs shut and there would be marks of force being used.'[4]

*Item*: In January 1982 a motorist called John Allen was convicted of raping a seventeen-year-old girl who hitched a lift with him after finding herself stranded after

a party. Fining Allen a paltry £2,000 instead of gaoling
him, Judge Bertrand Richards observed: 'The victim was
guilty of a great deal of contributory negligence.'[5]

The Fallen case took place against a background of increasing
public sympathy for rape victims and evidence of a frightening
rise in the number of reported cases of rape and attempted rape:
a 29 per cent increase in 1985 alone.[6] Public concern about these
figures, combined with a greater willingness on the part of police
to believe rape victims, has probably signalled to judges that sex
crimes now have to be taken more seriously than in the past. That
is not to say, of course, that every judge will in future examine
cases of rape and sexual assault from the same standpoint as Mr
Justice Rougier; his remarks are a welcome sign that things are
moving in the right direction, rather than evidence that the
problem no longer exists. In any case, the Fallen judgment dealt
only with one aspect of the relations between men and women,
that of coercive sexuality, and there is ample cause for concern
about the attitude of the judiciary to the role of women in other
areas of their relationships with the opposite sex. If you examine
the pronouncements of judges in a variety of cases—cases which
are absolutely unconnected, which take place in civil as well as
criminal courts, and cover a range of alleged transgressions from
murder to libel—an extraordinary theory emerges about the way
men and women are supposed to conduct their lives. Some of the
assumptions that used to apply routinely in the area of coercive
sexuality immediately come to light: most strikingly, the idea
that men live their lives on a hair trigger and can be provoked
to violence by the most insignificant stimulus, a notion which
parallels the old proposition that women must behave with circumspection at all times because of men's uncontrollable sexual
urges. But judges have gone much further than that, mapping out

exactly what type of behaviour is acceptable in a woman (particularly in a married woman) and what is not.

One of the most shocking events ever to take place in a British court was the trial of Nicholas Boyce for the murder of his wife Christobel at the Old Bailey in October 1985.[7] At the beginning of that year parcels of what appeared to be cooked meat started turning up all over London. One consignment was found in a carrier bag outside a branch of the McDonald's fast-food chain. On investigation, these proved to be the mortal remains of Christobel; her husband had killed her, filleted the flesh from her bones and cooked it so that it would look like someone's Sunday lunch—and all with their two small children still living in the flat where these events took place. He put her head in a bag and dropped it into the Thames from the Hungerford footbridge.

Journalist Maureen Cleave, writing in the *London Standard* after the trial, described the picture of the couple's life which she had pieced together by talking to Christobel's friends. It was one of a woman who had tried hard to save an unhappy marriage in which she had almost always been the breadwinner:

> Christobel was happy to do the coping. She never complained. She encouraged [Boyce] to do a doctorate at the LSE and when his grant ran out—for he was always in trouble with his tutor or his thesis—she worked as a geriatric social worker to pay his tuition fees as well as everything else. For most of their married life she was the sole provider. The lease of their flat was in her name.

Christobel wanted to live in the country, which her husband refused to do, and she had finally decided to leave him. She had found a house in Lavenham for herself and the two children, but she worried about how Boyce would manage by himself, and she agreed against her better judgment to spend Christmas 1984 with him. Even so, the signs were ominous; Christobel wrote to an aunt, saying she feared Boyce was planning to kill her. Two close friends of Christobel told Maureen Cleave they had asked to give evidence at the Old Bailey but were never called:

> They would have told the court how worried they had been about Christobel, how they begged her to spend Christmas with them; how their telephone conversations with her would end abruptly when apparently Nicholas came into the room; how she was frightened; how she had brought her few possessions to them in a box for safe keeping because he had begun to break things that were special to her, beginning with her watch; how he had been reading books about criminal law and, more sinister, about cot deaths.

Boyce's defence, at his trial, was that his wife was an impossible woman, a nag who provoked him into killing her. His barrister, Michael Wolkind, described his client as 'an exceptionally calm, patient and kind man who finally snapped and lost control'. Boyce was convicted of the lesser charge of manslaughter. The judge, Sir James Miskin, Recorder of London, addressed these remarks to him as he sentenced him to a mere six years in prison:

> Before these dreadful events you were hard-working, of good character, devoted to your children and a good father. You were simply unable to get on with your wife.

You stand convicted of manslaughter. I will deal with you on the basis you were provoked, you lost your self-control, and that a man of reasonable self-control might have been similarly provoked and might have done what you did.

Not only did you kill her, but you came to your senses, and took meticulous steps to ensure her death would never be discovered. You got rid of her body, you cleaned up the flat as best you could.

You cut her up with a saw and boiled her skin and bones. You bagged up her pieces, and over the next two days disposed of her body.

The picture of family life conjured up by this judgment is mind-boggling. Is it really the case that a man of 'reasonable self-control' could be so enraged by anything his wife said that he would kill her, cook her in their flat with their children in the next room, and dump her all over London? Is the average marriage a sort of uneasy truce in which both sides maintain a state of high alert and at least one is ready to wage total war at the least sign of discord? The notion that husbands are buffeted by gusts of aggression they cannot control, that their wives must at all times behave with circumspection to avoid provoking these uncontrollable outbursts, is as demeaning to men as the old idea that they are helpless victims of their sexual urges. The sexual analogy is apt; what Christobel really seems to have been 'guilty' of is undermining her husband's masculinity by usurping his role as chief provider and decision-maker for the family, which is exactly what a wife is supposed not to do. We are dealing here with old-fashioned images: the notion that a man's home is his castle where, regardless of what happens to him in the other—the *public*—part of his life, he is entitled to feel safe and in charge.

It is his wife's job to contribute to that feeling of security, not to undermine it by putting the castle in her name—or, worse, deciding to move out of it, as Christobel was preparing to do.

The Boyce case demonstrated that Sir James Miskin is a man with very clear ideas on the proper role of a wife. Another case which came before him, that of a man who was charged with murdering his wife's lover, gave him the opportunity to develop these ideas more fully.[8] Joseph Robb, a forty-one-year-old Canadian businessman, stabbed Michael Horton to death in a frenzied attack after flying to London in an attempt to talk him into giving up the affair. The two men met in a West End hotel in May 1987; when Horton turned down his pleas, Robb hit him first with a bottle of Perrier water, then with an unopened bottle of gin, and then stabbed him twenty-nine times with a penknife.

Robb and his wife Sheila had been married for twenty-two years. In 1981, Mrs Robb got a job with a public relations firm where Horton was general manager. She was good at her job and enjoyed her new independence; she started an affair with Horton, bought her own flat and told her husband she intended to leave him. It was at this point that Robb flew to London to see Horton.

In his summing-up, Miskin praised Robb's devotion to his wife and children. He remarked that Robb had been willing to allow his wife to get a job and exercise her 'bright little mind'. When Robb came to London, Miskin said, it had been in the hope that he might talk Horton out of 'a continuance of that disgusting affair'. Robb had also, Miskin said, hoped that his mother-in-law might be prevailed upon 'to try to dissuade Sheila from further idiocy'.

When Robb was cleared of murder and found guilty of manslaughter on the grounds of provocation, Miskin described the jury as 'sensible'. Sentencing Robb to three years for manslaughter, he said he was 'absolutely certain' that the businessman had not intended to kill Horton but had 'suddenly and completely lost self-control and launched that appalling attack'.

The most striking aspect of this case is the way in which it reveals Miskin's concept of a woman's role in marriage: permanent, inescapable, taking no account of her changed feelings or more mature preferences (Mrs Robb was still a student when she married). She is not, in other words, an independent creature at all. She has no right to work; if her husband allows her to do so, then that is simply evidence of his generosity. If his kindness is then flung back in his face, if she unaccountably decides she would prefer to live apart from him, it is only natural that he should seek to reassert his rightful control of her. And it is reprehensible, but not surprising, that a man faced with his wife's unrepentant lover should launch upon him a lethal attack. The model of male-female relations proposed here is clearly feudal in origin, implying ownership on the part of the husband and classing an extra-marital affair as a violation of property rights. Yet it was apparently acceptable not only to the judge and to Robb's QC, Richard Ferguson ('One of the most classic instances of provocation'), but also to the jury. The case raises, and leaves unanswered, this question: in what circumstances *can* a married woman leave her husband? We have been dealing, so far, with cases in which judges felt the need to articulate their disapproval of female conduct. In the summer of 1987 a case came to court which gave a judge a rare chance to express his ideal of womanhood. When Jeffrey Archer, the Conservative politician and best-selling novelist, sued the *Daily Star* for libel over an article alleging he had had sex with a prostitute, his wife Mary was called as a witness. She made a most favourable impression on the judge, Mr Justice Caulfield, as he made clear in his summing-up.[9] This is what he said:

Remember Mary Archer in the witness box. Your vision of her probably will never disappear. Has she elegance? Has she fragrance? Would she have, without the strain of this trial, radiance? What is she like in physical features, in presentation, in appearance? How would she appeal? Has she had a happy married life? Has she been able to enjoy rather than endure her husband Jeffrey? Is she right when she says to you, you may think with delicacy, 'Jeffrey and I lead a full life.'

They were married, if my memory is right, twenty-one years before the first Saturday of this trial, which was their anniversary. They are blessed, no doubt they would say, with two sons, who are possibly at their most attractive ages and interesting periods of thirteen and fifteen.

Though her husband is obviously busy and leads a careering political life throughout the country, he comes home at the weekends. A couple of days a week, Mary, who has great distinction in her own right, is in London, perhaps two or three days a week. So is there any abstinence from marital joys for Jeffrey Archer?

It is a deeply romantic picture of marriage and motherhood: the wife who is the heart of the family, a paragon who is able to minister to the needs of her children and her husband *and* maintain her own interests as well. Some of the adjectives—'fragrant', 'elegant'—conjure up a vision of a beautiful upper middle-class mother, her silk dress rustling as she visits the nursery to say goodnight to her children before disappearing in a waft of perfume, gliding from the house on her husband's arm to attend some glittering social function. They have a dated feel, a turn-of-the-century atmosphere, an Edwardian quality. The woman's sexuality is unthreatening, dedicated to its proper purpose, procreation and the very frequent (four or five times a week is implied) satisfaction of her husband's needs, occurrences which she naturally 'enjoys' rather than 'endures'; the ideal wife is always in tune with her husband's wishes. What Caulfield has in mind is an eroticized version of the Madonna, the possession of whom by her husband precludes the need for the Whore; she is sexy but not sordid, dependable both in her fidelity and in her implicit promise never to provoke desires she is unwilling to fulfil. This woman will never taunt, or complain, or take a lover; she has far too much delicacy to get involved in anything under-hand, or into a compromising situation. She is the upper-middle-class Englishman's ideal woman, an Edwardian dream, and she is the standard against which, unconsciously or otherwise, the rest of us are constantly measured. How can we hope to compare?

1 Information taken from report in the *Daily Telegraph*, 4 March 1988.

2 Report in the *Independent*, 13 January 1988.

3 Report in the *Hackney Gazette*, 21 March 1986.

4 Report in the *Sunday Times*, 12 December 1982.

5 Article in *Time Out*, issue 595, 15–21 January 1982.

6 Report in the *Daily Telegraph*, 14 March 1986.

7 Much of the information about the Boyce case comes from Maureen Cleave's excellent article in the *London Standard*, 'Epitaph for Christobel', 6 January 1986. Additional material is taken from reports in *The Times*, 3 and 10 October 1985.

8 Information on the Robb case from reports in the *Guardian*, *Independent*, and *Daily Telegraph*, 9 January 1988.

9 An edited version of the summing-up appeared in the *Daily Telegraph*, 24 July 1987.

# TOUCH ME

'SEXY SAM MAULED BY CAVAN "CAVEMEN" ' was the lead story in the *Sunday World*,[1] an Irish tabloid with a colour photo of a scantily clad model taking up most of its front page. It reported:

Topless model Samantha Fox had to cut short a dancehall date in Cootehill last week—after dozens of lusty Cavanmen invaded the stage.

The pint-sized page-three girl had to flee to her dressing room after a series of very determined advances by male fans who took the title of her hit song 'Touch Me' just a bit too literally.

Her bodyguards decided the show had to stop when they realised they could no longer guarantee her safety, according to tour promoter Cecil Thompson.

The scene at the late-night disco at the White Horse Hotel in Cootehill—one of 11 venues on a four-day Irish tour—was described by Samantha's father and manager, Pat Fox, as 'horrendous'.

A near-riot erupted when the crowd at the late-licensed disco became so excited that they burst through the protective ring of bodyguards and bouncers and on to the slightly raised stage where Sam was making her fully-clothed, non-singing public appearance.

The security guards included a former Mr Northern Ireland muscle-building champ, but they were no match for the fever-crazed Cavanmen.

When the fans began grabbing Sam's arm, kissing her hand and trying to clutch at her clothing, the organisers decided enough was enough.

They halted her scheduled half-hour show after only 20 minutes, and hustled an obviously shaken Samantha off to her dressing-room, leaving the crowd shouting for more.

One eye-witness said: 'I've never seen anything like it. There was never any question of Samantha appearing topless, or singing her hit song. All she was doing was smiling and answering queries about her career.

'But these guys got so worked up, they were practically pawing the ground and steaming through the nostrils. They were acting like a lot of cavemen.'

The DJ at the show added: 'It was sheer chaos. I don't mind admitting it—I was really, really scared.'

Despite attempts from some quarters to play down the seriousness of the incident, both Larne-based promoter Cecil Thompson and Samantha's father Pat agree that at one stage there was serious concern as to whether she'd escape from the melee unhurt.

Samantha Fox is the best known of the women who have made their living by posing with naked breasts in mass-circulation newspapers—the Page Three girls, who take their name from the page in the *Sun* newspaper on which the pictures first appeared. In common with most of them, she comes from a working-class background; her family lives in London and originally hails from the Republic of Ireland, where the riot described above took place. Her family has enthusiastically supported her career and her father Pat, who is also her manager, shrugged off the incident when he was interviewed by the *Sunday World*. 'She's used to scenes like this in the north of England, and it doesn't bother her,' he said. 'She's more worried about the safety of the fans.'

At first glance it seems a surprising statement. Samantha Fox is well below average height for a woman—she is around five feet tall. A short, slight woman who finds herself suddenly surrounded by a horde of frenzied men bent on touching her and grabbing her clothes could be forgiven for finding it at the very least an alarming experience. The possibility of sustaining physical damage, even sexual assault, might well cross her mind; to the outsider, it sounds frighteningly like the setting for a gang rape. But we are in the world of Page Three and that is, above all else, a world where nothing is as it seems. Sam's concern is not for herself but for her 'fans'; when the show was brought to a premature end her reaction, according to her father, was to feel 'sorry for all the people who'd paid to see her'.

Page Three girls—never women—do not think of themselves. Their aim is to please. Every day they smile and pout from their newspapers, no pose too contorted for them, displaying their readiness for sex. Breasts thrust forward, nipples already erect, there's no need even to bother with foreplay. They're here, they're undressed, they're excited, they're *ready*. The invitation is clear, just like Sam's hit song: come on, touch me, touch me now, you've paid your 25p.

None of this is true, of course, as you can see if you look closely at the photographs. The eyes remain curiously detached, the breasts are slung round the neck like fashion accessories, a scarf or necklace put on for the latest shoot (and, like them, a saleable commodity). These girls are here *to make money*. But that's the one thing their tabloid employers refuse to admit, no matter how many stories they carry (presumably *pour encourager les autres* as the current favourites age) about the wealth amassed by Samantha Fox or Suzanne Mizzi or Maria Whittaker. An essential part of the Page Three mythology is that the girls do it for the sheer love of showing off their bodies, because they really are panting for sex with the reader, whoever he happens to be—his age, looks, habits and personal hygiene have no bearing on the strength of her desire. The secret of Samantha Fox's success is her ability to act this part, to banish any suspicion that her motive isn't pure, as the text of *Daily Girls* No. 5,[2] a seedy colour booklet consisting of semi-nude photographs of her, makes clear:

> Sam has the ability to communicate through the camera. She's not posing into a lens, she is looking directly at you and me: everything that's going through her head is with us in mind. Just look at that face—those parted lips waiting to kiss the next man she sees, those eyes looking straight into yours. No cheesy grins, no pretending. She looks as though she wants to grab the man of her dreams—and right now, that man is *you*. Imagine those moist lips, kissing you all over. Think of that voluptuous body pushing up against you. Excited . . . ? So is she!

This is a fantasy of willingness: the Page Three girl is waiting 'to kiss the next man she sees'; she isn't pretending, she wants the man of her dreams and it's you, it's *you*. So seductive is its power that the real woman and the photographic image elide; Sam appears on stage in a carefully managed public appearance in Ireland or the north of England (more money in the bank and this time she doesn't even have to remove her clothes) and her 'fans' take her at face value. Hasn't she promised her compliance in a thousand newspaper pictures? So now she's here, why doesn't she deliver? Why has she arrived with an entourage of musclemen to hold back the crowds? That the daily contract they thought they had made with her has no enforceable meaning becomes clear only when they storm the stage and find themselves repulsed, the fantasy object whisked away. Or when they spot a Page Three girl in the street and shout to no avail—as reported in the *News of the World* by Maria Whittaker's ex-boyfriend— 'Get yer tits out!'[3]

The consumers of Page Three are, of course, perceived as male; the 'you and me' in the passage quoted above are 'the next man she sees', 'the man of her dreams'. But the pictures, while not directed at other women, cannot but affect them. Here the emphasis of the 'ordinariness' of the girls is significant; their working-class origins, referred to earlier, are emphasized in captions to reinforce the impression that they are the girls-next-door. This fiction is essential to the consumer's fantasy of availability: the average *Sun* reader will sense an unbridgeable gulf between himself and a duke's daughter or a university-educated fashion model, whereas a plumber's daughter from Preston or Tottenham seems within his reach. Of course Page Three girls aren't ordinary; few women share Samantha Fox's physical characteristics, and of those that do only a small minority are willing to display them in public. But the tabloids' insistence that Page Three girls are Miss Average has two baleful effects as far as other women are concerned. It fosters a myth that this model of sexuality—its passivity, its lack of demands on the male, and above all its *perpetual availability*—is what men are entitled to expect from all women. Second, and this is one of its more breathtaking effects, the popularity of Samantha Fox transforms an exaggerated image of the female form into a standard of female beauty. Ms Fox, by any objective judgment, is out of proportion. Her small body, well under average height for a woman, is dominated by a secondary sexual characteristic gone mad, a huge pair of breasts (requiring, apparently, a 38DD bra cup, whatever that may be) which constitutes a constant reminder of her biological role. Ms Fox can never know the freedom of going without a bra, without straps and painful bits that dig into the flesh—except, of course, when she is in front of the camera. Her chest relegates her to the position of the crudest of sex objects, one so lacking in subtlety that it is not hard to conjecture that her 'fans' are characterized by the immaturity and functional nature of their sexual response. Yet the popularity of Samantha Fox, Debee Ashby and Suzanne Mizzi is such that ordinary women come to feel that they, rather than the Page Three girls, are disproportionate or lacking in some way; tabloid newspapers even run stories about men giving their wives and girlfriends Christmas 'presents' of breast-enlargement operations at expensive private clinics.

It is the pressures which the existence of Page Three pictures in tabloid newspapers place on other women—their dishonest model of female sexuality, and their transformation of an atypical physical form into a standard for all—which have led to demands that they should be banned. Opponents of these demands have signally failed to tackle the real issue, preferring to ridicule and impute motives of envy and prudery to those who object to the pictures, particularly if they happen to be women. Clare Short, Labour MP for Birmingham Ladywood, has been accused of jealousy, by other MPs and by the press, for her attempts to introduce a bill which would remove Page Three girls from newspapers and confine them to specialist magazines. A report in the *Daily Telegraph*[4] by Godfrey Barker, following a parliamentary debate on Ms Short's bill, is typical; Barker littered his copy with schoolboy puns, observing that the troubles of Rupert Murdoch, proprietor of the *Sun* newspaper, had 'piled up breast-

high', as MPs voted 'to drop a figleaf on Page 3'. Then he went
for the MP:

> Miss Short, with a look that might have expurgated
> Robinson Crusoe, stared venomously at them [oppo-
> nents of the bill]. Her none-too-loosely-covered bosom
> rose and fell like the waters of the Hellespont.
>     'I think the Members opposite display their attitudes
> for all to see,' she spat out, so icy as to freeze the ink on
> the £1 cheques Mr Murdoch will now send inviting Miss
> Short to bare all in the *Sun*.

The irony of such attacks is lost on the likes of Godfrey
Barker, who appear incapable of understanding that Page Three
is, by its very nature, the antithesis of the erotic, denying all
possibility of reciprocity and reducing the male sexual response
to little more than a visually induced wank. It is Samantha Fox
and her father/manager, the men who photograph her, and the
newspapers that print her pictures, who espouse a fraudulently
'liberated' sexuality, extending an invitation which they have no
intention of fulfilling. I hope the Cavan 'cavemen' got their
money back.

1 *Sunday World*, 1 June 1986.
2 *Daily Girls* No. 5, published by Bunch Publishers Ltd, 14 Rathbone Place,
  London W1P 1DE.
3 *News of the World*, 7 February 1988.
4 *Daily Telegraph*, 13 March 1986.

# HE KNOWS
# HE CAN MAKE MONEY
# OUT OF YOU

The film director Brian de Palma once hit on the idea of making a movie about a sound recordist, played by John Travolta, whose job is to provide spine-chilling screams for a film he is working on. The scene for which they are required shows a naked woman being hacked to death in a shower—de Palma seems to have reacted rather literally to being dubbed the 'poor man's Hitchcock'. Various actresses are auditioned, their yells being stimulated by the simple expedient of pulling their hair, but none comes up to scratch. In the end, the effect Travolta is looking for drops into his lap in the shape of a tape-recording of his own girlfriend being murdered. He cheerfully re-edits the scene, substituting the 'real' screams for those of the actress in the shower, and everyone is happy.

*Blow Out* (1981) is just the sort of thing you'd expect from a director whose main claim to fame is the notorious slasher movie *Dressed to Kill* (1980), in which Angie Dickinson falls victim to a frenzied knife attack in a lift. But it also happens to catch perfectly what de Palma and his ilk are about: the marketing of female fear as a commodity.

Female fear sells films. It's a box-office hit. In 1960, the shower scene in Hitchcock's *Psycho*—Janet Leigh stabbed to death by Anthony Perkins—shocked audiences who had never seen anything like it on their cinema screens; today such scenes are ten a penny. Terror, torture, rape, mutilation and murder are handed out to actresses by respectable directors as routinely as tickets to passengers on a bus. No longer the stock in trade only of pornographers and video-nasty producers, they can be purchased any day at a cinema near you. Or, if you can bear to wait a few months, you can enjoy them in the comfort of your own home, courtesy of your local video emporium. *He Knows You're Alone*, *Bad Timing*, *The Night Porter*, *Body Double*, *Jagged Edge*, *The Shining*, *Fatal Attraction*; the list is endless.

What are we to make of this? Is it simply that a society inured to violent images by television requires bigger and bigger helpings of gore to raise a shiver? The popularity of Sylvester Stallone's films, especially the bloody *Rambo* series, suggests there is some truth in this explanation. And we are more *used* to real violence than we were twenty years ago; crimes which would have made headlines then are now so frequent that they are tucked away on the inside pages of newspapers. But the women who, as Peter Sutcliffe was put behind bars, picketed and even attacked cinemas in the north of England for showing films like *Dressed to Kill* and *He Knows You're Alone* (Armand Mastroianni, 1980) clearly felt the movies had a special relevance to the state of fear in which they found themselves.

They were right. The Stallone films, and war films like Clint Eastwood's *Heartbreak Ridge* (1986), do not break any taboos. There is no universal prohibition on men beating up other men in our society; the man who gets involved in the odd punch-up at closing-time is a bit of a lad; thousands of people turn up at the Albert Hall to watch two men pound each other to pulp in the name of sport. There are institutions—the army and, increasingly, the police—in which an aggressive male response is actually encouraged. Consequently, the man who leaves the cinema after watching *Rambo* (George P. Cosmatos, 1985) or *Cobra* (Cosmatos, 1986) doesn't take with him any ideas he didn't already have. This is not to say that the Stallone films do not have a pernicious effect; simple logic dictates that the glorification of violence as a weapon of first resort is likely to encourage the aggressive tendencies of young men who go to see them. Fortunately, the fantasy element in the Stallone films remains fairly evident. Rambo may be able to take on the entire Vietnamese army single-handed and come out on top; common sense warns the average man in Leeds or London that the outcome for him would be less certain.

Slasher films are a different matter. In spite of the dismaying frequency of crimes like rape and sexual assault, it is still conventional in our society to condemn sexual violence towards women. Yet this situation masks a massive ambivalence about violence that takes place in a sexual context. In his book *Order of Assassins*, Colin Wilson discusses a French novel called *L'Image*, a sadomasochistic fantasy after the model of *The Story of O*. In this book the heroine, Anne, becomes a sexual slave, just as O does; the novel ends with a scene in which she is whipped unconscious by another woman and then buggered by the narrator. Wilson writes: 'The relation between Anne and her "masters" is the normal sexual relation seen through a magnifying glass.'[1] Further into the same chapter, he goes on:

> It is important to bear in mind that there is nothing *basically* wrong with the male-female relation portrayed in *L'Image*, no matter what women's lib may say to the contrary. It is the normal male-female relation; this is why 'to do' a girl is one of the synonyms for possessing her; the male is the doer, the girl the 'done'.[2]

Wilson is a maverick; he loves to shock. But the passage is, unintentionally, a neat demonstration of the effect not only of books like *L'Image* but of slasher films like *Dressed to Kill*. Quite simply, they move acts of sexual violence from the sphere of solitary, unadmitted fantasy into the domain of shared experience. The viewer is no longer alone; those acts which he may have imagined privately, perhaps with a degree of shame, have also been visualized by the screenwriter, the director, the special effects man, and the hundreds of other people involved in the making of a film. And here, sitting in the seats that stretch in front and behind, are dozens of other men who have, like him, paid money to see them. Just as Colin Wilson reads about violent sexual acts being 'done'—his word—to a woman and in the process thinks they have been legitimized, someone who watches a naked woman being terrorized on her bed by a man with a knife may also conclude that such behaviour is 'normal'.

This impression is reinforced by the specifically sexual context in which the acts are performed. Constant references to 'ordinary', non-violent sexuality are used to confuse the meaning of what the viewer is seeing. There is the setting: often a bedroom or a shower, places strongly associated with the sexual act (in *Jagged Edge*, the victim is in bed; *Blow Out* repeatedly replays the murder in the shower); the clothes, or lack of them, of the victim (de Palma's female characters are always bursting out of low-cut blouses, regardless of the weather; they frequently wear miniskirts); even the behaviour of the rapist or murderer, which frequently mimics foreplay (Art Garfunkel caressing Theresa Russell's unconscious body prior to raping her in *Bad Timing*; Jeff Bridges drawing the knife across his victim's face in *Jagged Edge*). In one extraordinary case, *He Knows You're Alone*, the sexual act and violent death are implicitly equated. The plot concerns a young woman who is about to get married; on the eve of her wedding, she is stalked through the streets by a gaunt figure with a knife and turns to an ex-boyfriend, a pathologist who works in a morgue, for help. The film is essentially a race to see who will win her, the man with the knife or the boyfriend whose job is cutting up cadavers.

The sheer length of the violent scenes is evidence that, far from being incidental to the plot, a little piece of unpleasantness to be got out of the way as quickly as possible, they are integral to the message of the slasher movie. As well as being filmed with loving care—with shots from every conceivable angle, including directly above the action—they are often drawn out way beyond the needs of the story. *Blow Out* has a particularly ludicrous denouement: the kidnap and murder of Travolta's girlfriend, played by Nancy Allen, is extended to several minutes by a series of improbable devices, chiefly the killer's inexplicable determination to dispatch his victim only after he has dragged her to the top of a very tall monument in Philadelphia. Their ascent is painfully slow, hampered by the woman's attempts to escape, giving the audience plenty of time to relish her gasps, screams and anguished cries for help. Even so, de Palma, who wrote the film as well as directing it, seems to have been obsessed by his anxiety that it may yet fall short of some self-imposed quota of female fear. The story is actually to do with the cover-up of a political assassination, to which Travolta is an accidental witness while out with his tape machine to record wildlife noises; his job as a sound man is integral to the plot, but the complication about needing to find authentic female screams is a gratuitous addition to enable the film to start with a murder as well as end with one. (For the *cognoscenti*, an extra *frisson* is provided by the fact that Nancy Allen, who is pursued by a maniac in *Dressed to Kill* as well as in *Blow Out*, is put through these ordeals by a director who also happens to be her husband.)

Slasher films are vulgarly known as slice-and-dice movies, a term which at once ridicules them and belies their significance.

For these are films which come with a fully-formed ideology, one that has nothing to offer in the way of originality, but that is no less damaging to women for all that. Put baldly, their true theme, and a subject on which they display an extraordinary unanimity, is that women *deserve* to have these things happen to them. The women who are raped and murdered in slasher films are guilty in a variety of ways, starting with the directly sexual. *Body Double* (de Palma, 1984) is a good example: the victim provokes her savage murder by a sexual exhibitionism which takes the form of deliberately undressing in front of a lighted window every night. *Psycho*, the film which may justly claim to have laid the foundations of the genre, has much the same message, though more subtly done; it is Janet Leigh's sexually motivated criminal behaviour—the theft of $40,000 from her kind and considerate employer so she can run off with a married man—which puts her into the power of the murderous Norman Bates. (The film provoked one of Hitchcock's friends, Charles Bennett, into accusing the director of being a 'sadistic sonofabitch,'[3] a conclusion with which it is hard to quarrel. The stimulus for Hitchcock's sheer nastiness to women undoubtedly lies in his solitary and intensely Roman Catholic childhood. It erupted in even more pustulant form in his 1972 movie *Frenzy*, which contains one of the most graphic strangling scenes ever filmed.)

The reason why *Dressed to Kill* caused such anger was its dual implication that murder is a punishment for autonomous sexual behaviour in women, and that women actually *desire* sexual violence—thus legitimizing what is done to them and transferring guilt from the perpetrator to the victim. Given that women in the north of England had just spent several years in the shadow of the Yorkshire Ripper, it is hardly surprising that many of them were outraged. But *Dressed to Kill* went even further than that. The story, again written as well as directed by de Palma, starts

with Kate Miller (Angie Dickinson), an attractive woman troubled by erotic fantasies so violent she has sought help from a
psychiatrist, Dr Robert Elliott (Michael Caine). Driven by her
fevered imaginings, Kate picks up a man in an art gallery after
an elaborate and seductive game of cat-and-mouse, and goes back
to his flat to have sex with him. On the way out, she is attacked
and bloodily murdered in the lift of his apartment block. Kate's
distraught son then teams up with a prostitute, played by Nancy
Allen, to track down the killer—who turns out to be none other
than Dr Elliott, dressed up as the woman he longs to be. Thus
the crime is subtly transformed into a woman-to-woman affair,
motivated by jealousy, with no guilt attaching to the male characters (another echo of *Psycho*); indeed the clear message is that
it is the *female*—represented by the 'feminine' side of Elliott's
character—which is dangerous, not the male.

*Dressed to Kill* is, in essence, a crude response to male fears
aroused by the new model of sexuality claimed for women by
feminism. Kate, ostensibly a mature and attractive woman with
the confidence to act on her sexual desires, secretly wants mutilation and death. The de Palma films go on general release and
receive a measure of critical attention; nevertheless they occupy
a slightly fuzzy area between 'art' films and sleaze. *Jagged Edge*
(1985), made in Hollywood by an English director, the late
Richard Marquand, is in a different category altogether. An
upmarket thriller, it opened to wide acclaim which left Marquand all the more unprepared for the bitter complaints it provoked from many of the women who went to see it.

The film's central character is a cool and professional female
lawyer. Marquand seems to have gone out of his way to make
her as unlike the conventional Hollywood heroine as possible,
even to the point of finding an actress with an androgynous name
(Glenn Close) to play a character who is also ambiguously desig-

nated: Teddy Barnes. When we first meet her, reluctantly agree-
ing to defend a newspaper editor, Jack Forrester (Jeff Bridges),
who has been charged with the murder and mutilation of his
wife, her clothes are unprovocative, in tasteful shades of white
and cream to match her pale blonde hair. Everyone praises her
professional skills; it is clear we are shaping up for a courtroom
battle between Teddy and Krasny, the wily and untrustworthy
district attorney for whom she used to work as a junior prosecutor. Teddy is the only one who believes in Jack's innocence, but
she has another reason for taking on the case: she wants to atone
for her failure to speak up years before when Krasny sent an
innocent man to gaol by concealing vital evidence from the
defence.

So far so good; has Hollywood at last come to terms with
feminism? The answer is a resounding no, and the version of
reality which underlies Marquand's film has already been signalled by its staggering opening scene, a two-minute sequence of
nightmarish horror which only just stops short of showing a knife
ripping into a woman's flesh. When it begins, we are in a silent,
tastefully decorated beach house; the soundtrack consists of jan-
gling, disturbing music. The camera travels upstairs, giving a
brief glimpse of a man's outsize shadow on the white wall. We
are heading towards a pair of double doors, painted white like
the rest of the house. Suddenly a gloved hand reaches for the
doorknob and we are inside a bedroom where a woman in white
satin pyjamas is lying asleep under a white counterpane. She hears
a noise and begins to roll over; she is pinned to the bed by the
man's hand on her neck. We see the intruder for the first time—
masked, all in black except for his white gloves. He shows the
knife to the terrified woman, then slams it into the bedhead. He
feels in his pocket, produces a length of white cord, and proceeds
to tie her to the bed. She is struggling, whimpering, calling 'No!'

The camera moves in for a close-up of her anguished face. The man retrieves his knife, and runs it lovingly across her cheek. There are screams, and the camera suddenly takes up a position on the ceiling, looking down. In a parody of the sex act, the intruder straddles the trussed-up woman, ripping open her pyjamas to expose her breasts. The last thing we see is his long hunting knife moving down towards her naked body.

The scene is not in any sense necessary to the plot, even as a device to create dramatic tension. The film could just as well have opened with Jack, the husband who is accused of the murder, staggering out of the house after finding his wife's body and that of her maid, who has also been killed. But even when this terrible opening episode is over, Marquand is still unable to let it go. Within minutes, the camera is back in the bedroom, giving the audience a glimpse of Page Forrester's bloody corpse and the word 'BITCH' written in blood on the wall above her bed.

Now we come to Teddy. Once she has been established as a tough, cool, independent woman, Marquand sets out to undermine her in every way. He starts with her professional judgement: Teddy's reason for believing in Jack's innocence is shown as entirely emotional, based on her increasing attraction to him, while her male colleagues 'know', from their experience of human nature, that he is both guilty and very clever. In no time at all Teddy has gone to bed with him, turning herself into a guilty woman—much more so than when she'd merely let an innocent man rot in prison. The change is accompanied by a startling transformation in her wardrobe: her clothes suddenly move from virginal white to colour; in one scene, just after making love with Jack, she turns up in a slinky black bathrobe. By the time she arrives in court she is the embodiment of a particular sort of male fantasy, wearing tight business suits which accentuate her attractive figure. But she is also a bad mother, too busy to help her children with their homework even though their divorced father isn't on hand either.

The action grinds inexorably on, moving towards a conclusion that's obvious to everyone except the increasingly dense Teddy. She wins her case, largely by forcing a reluctant female witness to describe how she suffered an ordeal similar to Page Forrester's at the hands of a masked man who cut around one of her nipples and used her blood to smear the word 'BITCH' on the bedroom wall; when the woman finishes giving evidence, Teddy takes her hand and says a patronizing 'Well done'. The jury concludes, as Teddy has, that both this attack and the murder were carried out by an ex-boyfriend of Page. (She, of course, has turned out to have been sexually promiscuous; in other words, her death was a consequence of her own behaviour.) The case is hardly over before Teddy finds evidence concealed in Jack's house which proves his guilt. Instead of taking the sensible course— going straight to the DA—she embarks on a suicidally foolish (and, it's implied, *feminine*) course of action: she goes home, takes a shower, and admits the whole thing to Jack when he phones to ask why she left his house in such a hurry. Then she rings her assistant, Sam, but can't bring herself to tell him what she has discovered. Instead, she retires to bed, setting the scene for a reprise of the opening moments of the film.

Sure enough, here he comes; up the stairs, gloved hand on the door, now he's in the bedroom. Teddy is sitting up in bed in her white robe, just like a sacrificial victim. 'I want to see your face, Jack,' she says tremulously; at the last moment, as he approaches with the knife, she whips out a gun and shoots him.

It should be clear by now that *Jagged Edge*, far from being a feminist thriller, is precisely the opposite. Its purpose is the systematic demolition of a strong, independent female character in a way that reveals her to be sentimental, weak, and a bad mother to boot. It begins and ends with scenes of sexual sadism which would not be out of place in *Blow Out* or *He Knows You're Alone*. In making it, Richard Marquand did more than put a showy veneer on a shabby product; he turned himself into an occasional investor in the gilt-edged market in female fear. He did, however, leave an opening. At the end of the film the character played by Glenn Close has been shown up as a fool, a woman whose attempt to break into a man's world is doomed because her professional judgment is perpetually at risk of being influenced by her emotions. But she is, at least, still alive. In *Jagged Edge*, humiliation is the penalty for strong-mindedness in a woman, not death. It was left to another English director, Adrian Lyne, to take this anti-feminist theme to its logical conclusion, which he did in a film using the same actress, *Fatal Attraction* (1987). Here, the single career woman played by Close is not merely a professional rival of successful executive men, she constitutes a *physical* threat to the lover who has spurned her, and to his family. Michael Douglas, the hamster-jowled actor who plays the lover, Dan, insisted in an interview after the film was released that too much had been read into it; he said he was simply 'in the entertainment business. OK? I took on these roles [in *Fatal Attraction* and another film, *Wall Street*] because they're of interest to me; if they have a political message and lead to debate, that's good.'[4] But earlier in the same interview he became irritable as soon as the subject of feminist objections to the movie was raised:

> Look, the film isn't putting down single girls who have it all and want more, it just says that nasty things can happen. If you want to know I'm really tired of feminists, sick of them. They've really dug themselves into their own grave. Any man would be a fool who didn't agree with equal rights and pay, but some women, now,

juggling with career, lover, children, wifehood, have spread themselves too thin and are very unhappy. It's time they looked at *themselves* and stopped attacking men. Guys are going through a terrible crisis right now because of women's unreasonable demands. In my case I made *Fatal Attraction*, and the next thing is the feminists are ripping me apart and have interpreted it as a metaphor for all single women. My mind boggles at their arrogance.

It is hardly a coherent defence, either of Douglas's own position or of the film, first because he dismisses as 'women's unreasonable demands' a life-style that many men have historically taken for granted, and second because the film makes so scant an effort to work at a realistic level that it must be intended to be read metaphorically. The plot and characterization are full of holes: Alex, the spurned lover (another female character with a man's name, hinting at her role as usurper of male privilege; the choice is significant, though the intention may be subconscious), is two weeks into a new job as an editor with a high-powered New York publishing company when we meet her, yet she is able to take off as much time as she likes in order to harass Dan; in spite of her job, her apartment contains few books and she shows little interest in literature; she has no friends at all. Dan and his wife Beth are still madly in love after nine years of marriage, but one night's abstinence from sex—their daughter has decided to sleep in the marital bed—is enough to send him flying into the arms of Alex. Although it quickly becomes obvious to Dan that Alex is unhinged and may do some harm to his wife and child, he does not mention the affair to Beth until Alex has got into the house and boiled their pet rabbit. There is no evidence in the film that Alex has unusual manual dexterity, yet she is able to break into the couple's securely locked house and attack Beth in the bathroom. After Alex has been held under water in the bath for several minutes by Dan in an attempt to drown her she is still able to spring back into life until stopped by a bullet from Beth. The authorities then obligingly remove Alex's body, leaving the happy family to ponder over their narrow escape. Beth is not even taken in for questioning.

Far from being a naturalistic film, *Fatal Attraction* has several metaphorical meanings, all of which tend to reinforce traditional values and justify the annihilation of the independent woman who is the product of a century of female struggle. At its crudest propaganda level, the film's subject is the-nuclear-family-strikes-back; only the family unit, acting in concert, is able to counteract the destructive power of the single woman. At another, more figurative level, the film is about AIDS, and here is one of its larger dishonesties: the source of contagion, the carrier of the lethal virus to which Dan unthinkingly exposes his family, is located as a woman in spite of the fact that it was largely *men* who benefited from the relaxed morals of the 1960s which are implicitly under attack in the movie, and who passed on sexually transmitted diseases to their many sexual partners.

But there is another, very curious level of meaning in the film, and one which trails a persistently religious and magical significance. It is about things not being as they seem, about transformations, *transubstantiations* almost. This is not just because the stunningly attractive and liberated Alex turns out to be something far more sinister and old-fashioned, a denouement which is signalled early on in the film by the location of her flat in a converted warehouse above a meat market in the Hell's Kitchen area of New York, providing the director with a series of shots in which the approach to her apartment resembles a journey through the outer circles of the Inferno: visitors to the block hasten past suspended carcasses eerily lit by the glowing embers of braziers. (Would a single woman really choose this as a safe spot to return to late at night?) It is also the case that sex is transformed into violence, with the hurried and gasping couplings which begin the lovers' affair very little differentiated from their later breathless encounters as they throw punches at each other and struggle for possession of a kitchen knife. And water—a persistent motif from the opening shots of a water tower at sunset to Dan's failed attempt to drown Alex in the bath—is changed into blood. As Dan fucks her in the kitchen, Alex reaches behind to the taps, wets her hands and dampens their faces; moments later, when he insists on going home without promising to see her again, she puts her hands to his face and smears it with the blood from her slashed wrists. The power to transform, the power over the elements, is hers, not his—indeed, her seduction of Dan starts with a scene in which she, armed with a huge umbrella, offers him shelter from the pelting rain—and it is the key to understanding the film's otherwise nonsensical climax.

During the centuries when women were persecuted for being witches, for their supposed alliance with the devil, they were regularly put to the test by immersion in water. The theory behind the practice of 'swimming' witches was simple and brutal: if a woman came up to the surface and survived the ordeal, it proved her command of the black arts and she would be punished accordingly; innocent women stayed on the bottom and had to hope that their tormentors would pull them out of the water before they drowned. Alex, whose infernal nature has already been hinted at in the location of her flat, in her frizzy hair, in the cauldron which she uses to boil up the family's pet rabbit, and in her power over the elements (the water-into-blood motif suggesting a Black Mass), now bursts triumphantly from the water as Dan struggles to hold her under; she is a witch, the undrownable woman, the sorceress who ensnares unsuspecting men against their will—just as Circe used her spells to prevent Odysseus returning home from the Trojan War to his faithful wife Penelope. At a stroke Dan's guilt is wiped out and Alex stands condemned; it only remains for Beth, the wronged wife and mother, to carry out the vengeance which is rightfully hers.

And so the witch is dead, and in a manner which brings us full circle to *Psycho*, the start of it all. In Hitchcock's film (and, of course, in de Palma's *Dressed to Kill*) the murderer is revealed to be a man *dressed* as a woman, and in this way the 'feminine' part of a man is characterized as murderous, untrustworthy, to be resisted. *Fatal Attraction* takes this idea further; this time the killer really *is* a woman. The underlying theme of the slasher movie is now clear: it is women, the apparent victims, who are the true aggressors. If a man appears to take the initiative in violent acts, he is simply making a pre-emptive strike. Men beware women: the frills and furbelows of femininity hide the knife.

1 Colin Wilson, *Order of Assassins: The Psychology of Murder*, Panther, 1975, p. 71.
2 Ibid., p. 72.
3 Reported in John Russell Taylor, *Hitch*, Abacus, 1981, p. 238.
4 Interview with Val Hennessy in *You* (magazine of the *Mail on Sunday*), 6 March 1988, p. 20.

# HYPE, HYPE, HOORAY

*Presumed Innocent*, a first novel by the American writer Scott Turow, is every publisher's dream. In Britain, where most unknown writers count themselves lucky if they sell 2,000 copies in hardback, its sales climbed to 35,000 in months; the book received the prestigious Silver Dagger award from the Crime Writers' Association, being pipped to the top award of 1987 only by the hugely successful and long-established English novelist Ruth Rendell. In the United States, the paperback rights were auctioned for a staggering $3 million and the book has been made into a film. What is the secret of its success?

*Presumed Innocent* is the story not so much of a murder as of its aftermath. Its first person narrator, Rusty Sabich, is chief deputy prosecuting attorney in an unnamed city in the American Mid-West. Just as Rusty's boss comes up for re-election another member of the prosecuting staff, Carolyn Polhemus, is found raped and murdered in her apartment. Rusty is assigned to investigate the case and then, in a sensational development, finds himself charged with the murder. Much of the action of the book takes place in court, where Turow draws on his real-life experience as a lawyer to create a blow-by-blow account of Rusty's trial.

There is nothing new about this, nothing to explain the book's extraordinary sales figures: the courtroom drama has long been a staple ingredient of the crime genre, served up by novelists as diverse as Josephine Tey and Erle Stanley Gardner. But it is this element of the book that was chosen as a selling point by Turow's British hardback publisher, the upmarket imprint Bloomsbury (and picked up with enthusiasm by its reviewers). The blurb promises that the novel 'reverberates with shock and aftershock'; it is, it claims, 'a deeply provocative book about the ways of justice'.[1]

Yes and no. *Presumed Innocent* is a shocking book, but not because of what it has to say about American justice. In a highly politicized society like the United States, where everyone from the local dog-catcher upwards is elected and corruption has within recent memory spread its tentacles even into the Oval Office, it is hardly innovative to suggest that members of the police force, prosecuting service and judiciary might be venal. The truly disturbing thing about the book, even though it went unmentioned in the jacket blurb and in reviews, is the slow and calculated way in which it first reveals a widespread network of corruption and then locates its single source as—surprise, surprise—a glamorous, high-powered career woman. We are in the territory of the anti-feminist fightback.

Almost everyone in the book, including Rusty himself, seems at the outset a more or less normal human being. They have a few flaws—intense ambition, perhaps—but then they are politicians living in a sophisticated and morally complex society. They must be, in Turow's own phrase, 'presumed innocent'. But then, as the investigation gets under way, the facade cracks. Evidence of financial and sexual corruption starts to emerge. A file is missing, one which Carolyn had asked to see and which deals with allegations of bribe-taking among the prosecuting staff. Rusty is just getting his teeth into this aspect of the case, believing it might provide the motive for her death, when he is charged with the murder on flimsy and circumstantial evidence; the man who sanctions the charge is a political rival who has just beaten Rusty's boss, Horgan, in the election for chief prosecutor. Rusty discovers that Horgan has had an affair with Carolyn, then that his ex-boss intends to give evidence against him in spite of their years of working together. A crucial piece of evidence disappears. The black judge hearing the case, Larren, turns out to be yet another ex-lover of Carolyn. Even worse, Rusty discovers that Carolyn was deeply involved in the bribes scandal, and that Larren was her accomplice. Their guilt is bound to be revealed if the case continues.

It is hardly surprising, given the circumstances, that the judge soon halts the trial and Rusty walks free. This event is quickly followed by a series of hints that Rusty knows a lot more about the murder than he has so far admitted; the reader, whose sympathies have to date been enlisted on behalf of a baffled and obviously innocent man, is suddenly faced with the possibility that Rusty might be guilty after all.

He isn't, of course; what Turow has up his sleeve in the way of a denouement is far more sly and unpleasant than a re-working of Agatha Christie's famous early novel, *The Murder of Roger Ackroyd*, in which the narrator is dramatically revealed as the killer in the final pages. Turow's solution is an unusual one, a plot device I've encountered only once before in a fairly extensive acquaintance with crime fiction. Masako Togawa is a Japanese author and *chanson* singer; her novel *The Lady Killer*,[2] published in Japan in 1963, is the haunting story of a woman driven to madness and despair by the secret past she shares with her husband. He is Ichiro Honda, an attractive westernized Japanese, who makes a habit of picking up sad, unattached women in bars and going to bed with them, all the while taking elaborate pains to conceal his identity from his one-night stands. Suddenly his pickups start being murdered, and all the evidence suggests he is the killer, particularly the presence in their bodies of semen which reveals that he shares the same rare blood group as the criminal. Honda is convicted of the crimes, even confesses to them, and is saved from a death sentence only by the diligence of his lawyers. They discover that the real culprit is Honda's wife who, with the cunning of the deranged, has gone to immense pains to pin the murders on him. Because Honda is impotent with her (though not with other women), she has tracked down men with the same blood group through a blood bank, inveigled them into sleeping with her, and collected their sperm from her vagina. Then, having tracked down Honda's one-night stands, she has murdered them and injected the sperm into their corpses.

Give or take a few details, this is also the solution to the single rape-murder in *Presumed Innocent*; the murderer of Carolyn Polhemus is none other than Rusty's wife, Barbara. Her motive is jealousy, even though she does not find out about Rusty's affair with his colleague until it is over. She has collected Rusty's sperm from her vagina after sex with him and inserted it into the dead body of her rival, whom she has just murdered, to incriminate him. Whether her original intention was to pin the crime on Rusty, as in the Togawa novel, or simply to make him suffer when he is assigned to the case—which, since he is deputy chief prosecutor, is almost bound to happen—is not clear.

There is, however, a huge difference between Togawa's use of this device and Turow's. The couple in Masako Togawa's novel are trapped in a relationship in which love has been destroyed by guilt and despair; years before, they secretly conspired to kill and dispose of their hideously deformed newly-born child.

Their sex life is in ruins, Honda impotent and his wife suffering agonizing spasms whenever they try to make love. His solution is to seek solace elsewhere; denied any such outlet by her condition, and driven mad by guilt and jealousy, Honda's wife snaps and embarks on her plan of revenge. The reader feels pity and horror, as though a fissure has opened and offered a glimpse into hell, but draws no general conclusions from the tragedy.

The whole purpose of Turow's book, on the other hand, is to apportion blame. It is constructed as a series of revelations, stealthily luring the reader into the realization that everything that has happened, including Carolyn's murder, is the fault of one person and one person only, Carolyn herself. It is a lengthy piece of character assassination designed to strip away the glamorous veneer from the single, successful woman and expose the corruption underneath. As the book opens, with Rusty and Horgan on their way to Carolyn's funeral, we learn that the dead woman was a 'smart, sexy gal. A helluva lawyer.'[3] The rest of its 431 pages amounts to a systematic dismantling of Carolyn's character until, at the end, she stands revealed as a power-hungry bitch who slept her way to the top and didn't care whose feelings she trampled on. All the sins committed in the book turn out to have her as their instigator, whether it's Rusty cheating on his wife or the judge taking kickbacks from defendants many years before. She is a bad mother who neglected her son and does not deserve the affection he still feels for her. She has slept with almost every man in the case, and their sexual involvement with her is the catalyst which initiates other, deeper forms of corruption; it is as if her voracious sexual desire is a worm which lays in its victims the eggs of a whole host of maggots. It is precisely this process which leads to her death: her passing fancy for Rusty saps his moral strength and leads him into a double betrayal of his wife,

first by having an affair with Carolyn and then by revealing it
to her even though it is over. For Rusty, Barbara is as much a
victim of Carolyn as anybody else and the thought of turning
her in to the authorities scarcely enters his head. When their
marriage subsequently breaks up, it is at Barbara's insistence, not
his.

But why does Carolyn do all these things? This is the question at the heart of the book and it is one Turow has no difficulty
in answering. She is a woman in a man's world, a milieu in which
she should be at a disadvantage and yet is not, simply because she
is willing to exploit the one characteristic her male colleagues do
not share—her seductive female sexuality. Worse, she uses that
sexuality in a way that puts even her superiors—Rusty, Horgan,
the judge—in her power; she is a divisive, confusing presence in
the office, a repository of concealed knowledge, a manipulator of
pillow-talk secrets, a smart operator whom men helplessly desire
against their better judgment. The notion that Carolyn is an
intruder, a usurper, is reinforced by the fact that there are surpris-
ingly few female characters in powerful positions in the book:
it is peopled largely by male prosecutors, police, experts, reporters
and politicians. (Among the minor characters, women pop up
chiefly in stereotyped roles, the embittered spinster or the domi-
neering wife; Rusty describes them in phrases which unconsciously project on to them his own sense that the sexes are
perpetually at war. His secretary, Eugenia, is 'obese, single, mid-
dle-aged, and, it often seems, determined to get even for it all.'[4]
One of the witnesses against Rusty at the trial, Mrs Krapotnik,
is a widow: 'She does not say what Mr Krapotnik died from, but
it is hard to believe that Mrs Krapotnik was not partly the
cause.'[5]) Apart from Carolyn, the only woman in the book who
holds any significant professional position is another prosecutor

who, having killed her first husband in an accident caused by her drunken driving, is now confined to a wheelchair; she has been forced into a physical withdrawal from competition with her male colleagues and her sexuality, although she is still capable of bearing children, is no longer on threatening display in the way that Carolyn's is.

The book's real theme is an increasingly familiar one, that women's power is always achieved illegitimately and at the expense of men, and sometimes at the expense of other women. That being the case, Turow implies, female intrusion into public life—into *male* areas of life—inevitably brings with it the risk that violence will ensue. *Presumed Innocent* ends with Rusty promoted to his boss's old job, and Barbara setting off to start a new life in a new city. No one is punished for the murder of Carolyn Polhemus. But the book *is* about justice of a sort, with Rusty, flawed as he is, nevertheless representing an old-fashioned, non-party ideal of integrity and fairness; his failure to act makes clear that, in the book's terms, justice *has* been done. The true culprit, the real cause of the crime at the heart of the novel, is the dead woman herself; not just death but agony, terror and humiliation are her penalty.

Very near the beginning of the book, as his investigation gets under way, Rusty is shown the scene-of-crime pictures from Carolyn's apartment. His first sensation on seeing the body of his former lover is sexual excitement stimulated by her 'erotic bearing'.[6] Then he describes what he sees: the woman's body is naked and covered with bruises, and she has been tied up so that she arcs backwards in the shape of a bow. Her face is 'ghastly'; her eyes, because of attempted strangulation, are 'enormous and protruding'; her mouth 'is fixed in a silent scream'. Her look 'holds the same wild, disbelieving, desperate thing that so frightens me when I find the courage to let my glance fix on the wide black eye of a landed fish dying on a pier'. But as Rusty gazes at this tortured corpse, this vision of horror, what does he feel? 'Satisfaction.'

> Carolyn Polhemus, that tower of grace and fortitude, lies here in my line of sight with a look she never had in life. I see it finally now. She wants my pity. She needs my help.

Who needs rubbish like this?

1 Scott Turow, *Presumed Innocent*, Bloomsbury, 1987 (Farrar, Straus & Giroux, 1987).
2 Masako Togawa, *The Lady Killer*, Penguin, 1987 (Dodd Mead, 1986).
3 Turow, op. cit., p. 8.
4 Ibid., p. 47.
5 Ibid., p. 261.
6 All remaining quotes, Turow, pp. 28–9.

# THE FROG PRINCESS

There is a Regency romance by Georgette Heyer[1] in which the hero, the wealthy and fashionable Mr Beaumaris, is the most eligible bachelor in London. He is the natural successor to Beau Brummell, a figure so powerful that Society careers can be dashed merely at the raising of his eyebrow. His houses, his horses, his mistresses, are equally famous; his most recent inamorata, an exotic creature known only as 'the Faraglini', is a tempestuous beauty who flounced off to Paris as soon as their liaison came to its stormy end. But, glamorous and sophisticated though he undoubtedly is, Mr Beaumaris is an unhappy man. The charms of his mistresses have palled, and he is just as bored with those Society girls with whom he might properly make a match; he has been 'hunted by every trick known to the ingenuity of the female mind'.[2]

This world-weary hero has retreated to his Leicestershire hunting-box for a rest when a carriage happens to break down outside his front door. Inside is Miss Arabella Tallant, seventeen years old and fresh out of the nursery of her father's Yorkshire parsonage where she has been assisting her mother in the task of bringing up her numerous younger brothers and sisters. Arabella is on her way to London to take part in the Season; she is a fresh, charming *ingénue*, and it does not take long for her to capture the heart of the cynical Mr Beaumaris. It is a perfect Heyer romance, the union of youth and (relative) age, innocence and experience, genteel poverty and untold wealth. Its inevitable denouement—the couple's engagement—is delayed only by a plot device which requires Arabella to keep up an increasingly desperate pretence that she, too, is in possession of a fortune, a predicament from which she can be rescued only by someone of fabulous wealth, which is to say Mr Beaumaris. The book ends with the lovers sorting out the confusion, Mr Beaumaris admitting that he has known all along that Arabella is far from being an heiress. He kisses her, she sheds a tear, then 'she became tolerably composed, and was able to sit down on the sofa beside him, and to accept from him the glass of tepid milk which he told her she must drink'.[3] It is an unconsciously knowing touch on Heyer's part, for it is clear throughout the book that Arabella is as innocent as a babe and that this constitutes much of her charm for Mr Beaumaris. What appears at first glance to be a harmless romance is really something rather sinister: Arabella is valued by Mr Beaumaris for her childlike qualities—her dependence, her ignorance, her inexperience, her lack of adult status. Above all, she is a victim of the double standard which holds that the sexual adventures which enhance the standing of a Mr Beaumaris are absolutely forbidden to the woman he marries. She is a child-woman, unknowing prisoner of a fantasy whose bars she will feel as soon as she tries to extend her horizons. What will happen when she grows up is something about which we can speculate—almost inevitably, marital discord—but we do not discover it from Heyer. This is a fairy tale as well as a romance, and it is a convention of both genres to leave the couple to live happily ever after.

In 1980, much of the population of Britain became caught up in another fairy tale, this time the romance between Prince Charles, thirty-two-year-old heir to the throne, and a nineteen-year-old girl, Lady Diana Spencer. This is how Robert Lacey described events in his book *Princess*, a royal scrapbook for the simple-minded:

> Once upon a time there was quite an ordinary girl who became a princess. It is a short story, and very simple. She fell in love with a prince and he, warmed by her affection, fell in love with her. When the world found out about it, everyone rejoiced. Loyal subjects in tens of thousands thronged the streets to cheer her on her wedding day. The Archbishop of Canterbury, dressed in shimmering silver, compared this young girl's story to a fairy tale, and no one could seriously quarrel with that comparison.[4]

For John Pearson, in his book *The Ultimate Family*, the romance was 'a novelettish situation':

> For almost every detail of her life added to a picture of an up-to-date Cinderella, noble yet humble, acquainted with palaces but living a very humdrum private life, virginal but absolutely ready now to be awakened by her Prince's love and totally transformed.[5]

One romantic author was so enraptured by events that she actually did turn them into fiction: Mary Christopher's *Royal Wedding* is about a young American journalist, Julie Elliott, who comes to London to cover 'the most dazzling event of the decade!' and falls in love with her English photographer, Nick Tregarron. But things go badly:

> Even as the handsome photographer opened the most exclusive doors in England to her, he mocked her with

his cynical comments. Did he really think her no more than a silly, starry-eyed young American reporter? Didn't he realise that, like Lady Diana, Julie was ready for love?[6]

No need to hold your breath; he did. The novel ends with the aristocratic Nick producing a family heirloom from his pocket, an emerald ring handed down to him by the Dowager Lady Ardon [sic]. 'How thrilled,' Julie reflects poetically, 'the Elliotts would be to have the future Viscount Ardon in their family tree.' The lovers stand entwined on, of all places, the Hungerford footbridge over the river Thames:

> In the distance was the floodlit dome of St Paul's Cathedral, where earlier that day they had witnessed the marriage of Prince Charles and Lady Diana Spencer. Their Royal Highnesses would now be safely at Broadlands, the big country house where they were spending the first two days of married life, but Julie thought they couldn't be any happier than she and Nick were at that moment.[7]

The novel ends there; unfortunately for the Waleses, life carried on. Or, to put it another way, real life intruded. Diana, still only a startlingly inexperienced twenty-year-old, began to discover the confines of the role allotted to her by the press and by the horde of 'royal watchers' who make their living by exploiting the scant information available about the private lives of members of the royal family; everyone wanted a sequel to the Waleses' first, highly successful blockbuster, and it was a demand almost impossible for them to meet. The journalists who had revelled in the Royal Romance, quickly followed by the Royal Engagement and the Royal Wedding, had whetted an appetite that, perversely, grew rather than diminished in proportion to the

nourishment it received. Robert Lacey's *Princess* provides a fla-
vour of the part Diana was now expected to play:

> In less than a year this girl has become part of every
> British family, the relative everyone knows, loves and
> gossips about fondly, even if she never actually comes to
> call—an emblem and mascot that is fiercely cherished.[8]

What is an emblem supposed to do? How is she to spend her
time? This is Diana the prisoner of a thousand royal walkabouts,
condemned to pass her days in a numbing state of arrested development. In effect, her role is that of an animated tailor's dummy,
a focus for the nation's 'good feelings', a waxwork with a smile
perpetually fixed upon its lips. She is the property of the public,
and more crucially that of the public's representative in these
matters, the press. Even so, it might be thought that Diana now
carried out her limited duties with admirable expedition, becoming pregnant within four months of marriage, had this event not
coincided with something altogether less congruent with her
cloyingly feminine image: her first break for freedom. Amid
stories of rows with Charles and rebellions against the demands
of royal protocol, Diana began to emerge as a person rather than
an image. It was apparent that she was becoming aware of her
own needs, making demands on Charles, and reacting with irritation to the unrelenting gaze of reporters and photographers. In
other words the blushing bride, the 'shy Di' beloved of the
newspapers, had begun to grow up; part of the process was
discovering that her own wishes and those of her husband and
public did not always coincide. This was a far from unwelcome
development for journalists, who were able to get the best of both
worlds, denouncing an entirely predictable turn of events in
shocked tones and at the same time making the most of it in

column inches. After all, the bad-tempered Princess was a story with much more mileage in it than her previous pallid incarnation. Reports of royal conflicts, however tenuous their basis in reality, also fitted nicely with the newspapers' concept of the continuing saga of the Waleses as a real-life soap opera. Reporters delighted in transforming Diana from diffident teenager to nagging wife, regaling the public with tales of her moods, her impatience, and her inability to get on with the Queen. Fleet Street was in full cry, sold millions of papers and, in an unprecedented development, found itself summoned to Buckingham Palace and requested to give the Princess a breathing space. To little avail; Diana had been married for only eighteen months when one writer announced to her readers that the Princess was 'a spoiled brat', and another told an American television audience that she was 'a monster'.[9] Newspapers claimed she was a spendthrift, hard to get on with, incapable of keeping staff, that she had driven away Charles's friends, that she was anorectic.

That Diana had been the victim of a fantasy which had become outmoded even for the royal family was brought home in March 1986, when Buckingham Palace announced the engagement of the Queen's second son, Prince Andrew, to twenty-six-year-old Sarah Ferguson. If the bouncy and slightly vulgar Fergie had any parallels in art or culture they were to be found not in romantic novels but in those fleshy ladies who sprawl unselfconsciously across many a Rubens canvas; her celebrated lack of dress sense, which formed the basis of dozens of newspaper and magazine articles, was actually the consequence of an exuberant sexuality which demanded nudity as its natural form of expression. She simply would not fit into a Heyer novel, and no one seems to have thought of putting her there; from the beginning, Fergie's public image and real life were never far apart. On the very day of the engagement, for instance, the *London Standard* reported

that Sarah's 'most serious romance' before Prince Andrew was
with a forty-eight-year-old widower, Paddy McNally:

> Now a motor-racing consultant, he used to manage ex-
> Formula One world champion Niki Lauda. He went out
> with her for about three years.
>
> Sarah often used to stay with McNally in his beauti-
> ful chalet in Verbier, Switzerland, and she became very
> fond of his children.
>
> The relationship ended last year when she realised
> that it was unlikely to lead to marriage.[10]

Although it was not fully spelled out, the meaning was
unmistakable: Prince Andrew's bride *was not a virgin*. The unthinkable appeared to have happened; it was as if Mr Beaumaris's
best friend had suddenly announced that he intended to hurry to
Paris and propose to the voluptuous Faraglini. In fact, all the
marriage really signalled was the reluctance, in the late twentieth
century, of even close relatives of the Queen to sacrifice themselves to a publicly cherished but privately neglected romantic
ideal. (Princess Margaret, three decades before, had shown herself
more amenable.) With hindsight, the press should have looked
back with gratitude on Lady Diana's extraordinary patience in
accepting, for a few months at least, the impossibly old-fashioned
role they had invented for her.

But they didn't. Attacking the Princess of Wales had become
the tabloids' favourite sport, and in autumn 1987 the state of the
Waleses' marriage became a total obsession. Reporters who, as a
profession, are scarcely renowned for marital fidelity and a clam-
like attachment to home and family, observed that Diana and
Charles seemed to be spending a considerable amount of time
apart. The burning question, according to *Sun* journalist Judy

Wade, was: 'Had the world's most famous marriage lost its magic?' In her book *Inside a Royal Marriage*, which is rather short on information about its ostensible subject, Wade does at least record the way in which the press now fully reversed its original assessment of Diana:

> The commentators who had once got carried away describing how cleverly Diana had saved the Wales [sic] now decided it was all her fault. She was hardly a brilliant match mentally for a man educated to be a king, they noted. She had failed her O-levels not once but twice, he on the other hand, had left Cambridge with a second-class history degree. What could this couple possibly have in common?
>
> Diana had always mixed with a group of Super-Sloane friends who apparently had little interest in world affairs, her critics pointed out. Her husband had been influenced from birth by men of maturity and experience. Everyone knew that Charles looked on Sir Laurens van der Post as his own personal guru. While she loved to curl up with slushy novels or books about herself, her husband got stuck into anthropology, architecture or reports on inner-city slums.[11]

The curious feature of these charges is that Diana was coming under attack for aspects of her personality which *hadn't* changed. It was as if Fleet Street suddenly discovered it had been conned, that 'shy Di' was nothing but a dumb blonde, and chagrined reporters set out to get their revenge. But Wade's reference to Diana's alleged habit of reading books about herself is revealing; it is clear from reports around this time that one reason for the newspapers' hostility to Diana was her enhanced sense of self, the confidence that attached to her greater age, poise, and experience, and which unfriendly journalists interpreted as her arrogance. Once again the Prince was presented as a long-suffering, hen-pecked husband, but this time the papers didn't pull any of their punches. Charles was said to be sickened by his wife's dirty jokes and vulgar companions, with the *News of the World* claiming that a 'grim-faced' Prince had walked out of a dinner party after one of Diana's friends made a puerile but not particularly offensive joke ('What smells worse than an anchovy? An anchovy's bottom'). It announced first that the couple's differences were so great that they could barely contrive to be civil to each other, then that 'Charles and Diana are not speaking'.[12] The Prince, the paper reported, was spending time at Balmoral with his 'long-time confidante Lady Dale Tryon', whom he was said to have described as the only woman who understood him. The implication, that Diana's unreasonable behaviour had driven Charles into the arms of another woman, was obvious. The following day the *Sun* ran a front-page article repeating the story in the form of a denial, quoting the protest of Lady Tryon's husband: 'MY WIFE'S NOT PRINCE CHARLES'S LOVER'.[13] One newspaper broke with tradition by publishing an unflattering cartoon which portrayed Diana as a sharp-chinned shrew. Others dropped clear hints about Diana's 'infidelity', printing pictures of an Old Etonian banker who had apparently escorted her to various functions. Unlike Fergie, Diana was not going to be allowed to get away with even an imaginary affair; sexual inexperience, except with her husband, is the hallmark of the child-bride, and the development marked the ultimate step in Diana's fall from grace, the final detail needed to demonstrate her miserable failure to conform to the behaviour everyone had a right to expect of her. Six years on, the transformation was complete: white into scarlet, blushing bride into wicked lady, a new role for Diana that had as little foundation in reality as her original one.

Charles himself did not escape criticism for the alleged rift in the marriage, especially in the Murdoch papers, which regard him as an opponent of the Thatcherite policies they themselves espouse. But the brunt of the hysterical coverage was borne by Diana, as the journals which had worked hardest to imprison her in a child-woman fantasy simultaneously castigated her for making even a partial escape—the life led by the Princess of Wales is still hardly that of an autonomous, independent adult—and benefited in circulation terms from the dream's inevitable collapse. They even struck sanctimonious attitudes about it, at the same time hardly bothering to disguise their delight in the story and jostling to plumb new depths of tastelessness (the *Daily Star* invited its readers to phone in and vote as to whether or not Charles was having an affair with Lady Tryon). Hard-boiled hacks presented themselves as romantics, big old softies who believed every word they had written about the Royal Romance—gave the impression, even more implausibly, that they were avid consumers of slushy novels to whom it had simply never occurred that things might go wrong if the existence of the protagonists was prolonged beyond its natural boundary, the embrace on the final page.

Yet it was always apparent, even during their courtship, that Charles and Diana were being created in the image of characters in fiction, that they were participants in a fragile fantasy which bore the warning of its own sell-by date. The union of youth and age, innocence and experience, is an unequal and therefore an unstable one; it is a teacher-pupil relationship in which one partner is bound to change and the other is not. Diana could not go on being Arabella, even though Charles had long ago settled happily into the role of Mr Beaumaris. Her awakening, her abandonment of the colourless virtues of 'shy Di' in favour of the positive and negative characteristics of a grown-up woman, may well have taken her by surprise, for back in 1980 the sheltered Lady Diana Spencer—step-granddaughter, after all, of another romantic novelist, Barbara Cartland—was of all the characters in the drama least well equipped to appreciate the unreality of the situation in which she suddenly found herself. But the press had no such excuse, and the spectacle of Fleet Street making moral and financial capital out of the demise of the dream they foisted upon her is an unedifying one. There is a general lesson to be learned here, a moral about the folly of trying to act out a tinsel fantasy which denies adult status to women, but it is also a cautionary tale about journalists, about a princess who was kissed by Fleet Street and turned into a frog.

1 Georgette Heyer, *Arabella*, Pan, 1964.
2 Ibid, p. 55.
3 Ibid, p. 246.
4 Robert Lacey, *Princess*, Hutchinson, 1982, p. 8.
5 John Pearson, *The Ultimate Family: the Making of the Royal House of Windsor*, Grafton, 1987, pp. 379–80.
6 Mary Christopher, *Royal Wedding*, Bantam, 1982, back cover blurb.
7 Ibid, p. 179.
8 Lacey, op. cit., p. 126.
9 Quoted in Pearson, op. cit., pp. 390–1.
10 *London Standard*, 19 March 1986.
11 Judy Wade, *Charles and Diana: Inside a Royal Marriage*, Angus and Robertson, 1987, pp. 4–5.
12 *News of the World*, 18 October 1987.
13 *Sun*, 19 October 1987.

# IMMACULATE MISCONCEPTIONS

The Virgin Mary, you may recall, had very little choice in the matter. Someone turned up, implausibly claiming to be the angel Gabriel, and announced she was going to have a baby. Understandably surprised, Mary asked the obvious question: since she was still a virgin, how was this supposed to happen? After a singularly vague explanation involving another spectral visitor, this time the Holy Spirit, poor old Mary gave in. 'I am the Lord's servant,' she said meekly, 'as you have spoken, so be it.'[1]

The most interesting feature of this affecting little tale, which is related by the apostle Luke, is the resignation with which Mary accepted her fate. Perhaps it was because she was poor, not a Roman citizen, and living in a far-flung corner of the empire; other women of the period—the reign of the emperor Augustus—were less inclined to regard the news of an unplanned pregnancy with such stoical resignation. Abortion was widely practised in Rome and was not illegal in classical law. A great deal of contraceptive advice was also available, ranging from the ineffective (tying a cat's liver to your left ankle, which could have worked only by putting both parties off their stroke) to methods familiar to the twentieth century (introducing materials, such as wool soaked in honey, into the vagina as a barrier to conception; there is even some evidence that goats' bladders were used as a rudimentary and expensive form of condom). If a woman was unlucky and her chosen method failed, she was able to resort to abortion without fear of the criminal law, although her action might constitute grounds for divorce.[2]

It was not until the late second century AD, by which time the Roman empire was going downhill, that abortion became a punishable offence. The penalty was temporary exile; the specific crime was *not* murder—the foetus never had the status of a person in Roman law—but that the woman had 'cheated her husband of children'. The situation got progressively worse as Christianity established itself and Byzantium took over from Rome: abortion became an increasingly serious offence, the woman being deemed guilty first of theft, then of theft and murder. By the ninth century, the outlook for the unwillingly pregnant woman was grim.

Not so, in theory, for the Virgin Mary. Back in the first century BC, abortion, though frowned on by moralists like the orator Cicero, who fretted (rather like Sir Keith Joseph in the 1970s) about the middle and upper classes failing to breed, was nevertheless increasingly widely available. You might think, in fact, that Mary was precisely the sort of person who would avail herself of the services of the local wise woman: single, pregnant in extremely dubious circumstances ('You saw a *what*? Pull the other one!'), and with a fiancé who was doing his best to slide quietly out of his obligations (only an opportune visit from yet another heavenly emissary persuaded him to do his duty). Instead, Mary simply put up with it. Why?

Actually, we don't know that she did. If Mary raised strong objections, it would hardly have suited Luke's purpose to record the fact—the story performs too important a function within the Christian religion to allow any doubts to creep in. The Annunciation gives women a role in what is otherwise a male-dominated tale, and it is one which provides them with a nice, passive example to follow. Mary is nothing more than a receptacle, a useful vessel, but she will be cherished, admired, and even (in the more Mariolatrous houses of the Christian Church) worshipped as long as she stays in line. Her very place in history is contingent on her docility.

The story of the Virgin Mary and the angel Gabriel exemplifies women's role as perceived by Christian theology. It is one which is no less biologically determined than that offered by Freud, and it explains the peculiar terms in which abortion is discussed in our supposedly Christian society. Every time there is an attempt to limit access to abortion or end it altogether—and there have been plenty since the passing of the 1967 Abortion Act—those people who want to change the law suffer a bad attack of the Annunciation syndrome. It goes like this: 'Well, little lady, you can forget all those things you were planning to do with your life over the next few years—you've been chosen, you're going to have a baby! Isn't *that* nice! Come along now, no moaning, we don't want to hear about you not wanting children just yet, or how you'll lose your job (you won't be needing it anyway, not any more), or how you're living on social security and don't know how to cope, or your husband's run off with another woman—YOU'RE GOING TO BE A MOTHER.'

What the anti-abortionists are saying, in essence, is that the act of becoming pregnant, even if unintentional, strips a woman of rights which other people take for granted: the right to plan her life and to establish her own priorities. It is a denial of her status as an independent human being, returning her to a state of childlike subservience in which other people decide what she may and may not do. Her wishes, her desires, her aspirations, become conditional; meanwhile the foetus inside her body, a bundle of cells incapable of independent existence and for which, in many cases, she has not accepted responsibility (might even have, probably, done everything in her power not to bring into being), is accorded rights which take precedence over hers.

Of course, the argument is not addressed in these terms by the anti-abortion lobby. It suits their purpose in this case to insist on an inalienable right to life, even though at other times—on the question of capital punishment, for instance, or Britain's right to defend itself against the Russians by stockpiling weapons of mass destruction—this same right is explicitly or implicitly denied. (The hypocrisy of many anti-abortionists was neatly demonstrated by one of their own newspaper adverts during the campaign by the Liberal MP, David Alton, to make abortions illegal after eighteen weeks of pregnancy. The text trumpeted that the death penalty had been abolished for murder, and asked why it should be allowed for foetuses; prominent among the signatories were a number of people who have argued for the *return* of capital punishment.) This right to life, claimed on behalf of something which is not yet a viable human being, is posed against a list of the 'reasons' for which, it is claimed, women seek abortions. During the controversy over the Alton bill, it was alleged that women frequently demand terminations because they wish to go on exotic holidays or buy glamorous clothes. Put in those terms, the moral question looks black and white: a child's life weighed against the selfishness and frivolity of its mother. The scenario is, of course, an invention; most women decide to have abortions reluctantly, and with trepidation, as the lesser of two evils. No woman has an abortion for *fun*. They do not see why they should take on the responsibility of an unwanted child after their method of contraception has let them down; their families are complete and they do not wish to raise another child; their circumstances—bad housing, lack of money, ill health—are such that they cannot cope with a new baby; or they are aware, after having various tests, that the baby will be severely handicapped. These are *responsible* reasons for deciding to end a pregnancy, which is precisely why they are ignored by anti-abortion organizations; the image of mature, adult women weighing up the pros and cons and coming to their own decisions simply doesn't fit with their view of women as flighty, irresponsible creatures who can't be left to make up their own minds. It is much harder to refuse a termination if you accept that the person requesting it is an adult who has arrived at her decision after careful reflection; safer to stick with the ideology of the Annunciation syndrome, which rests on the premise that members of the female sex are weaker vessels, never quite grown up, tall children in fact, who need to have all major choices made for them. Good old Mary; when Gabriel turned up, she simply accepted that he knew best, at considerable inconvenience to herself. How galling it must be for the anti-abortion lobby that so few modern women believe in angels.

1  Luke 1:26–38.
2  Excellent accounts of the availability of contraception and abortion in the classical period are contained in the following books: Eva Cantarella, *Pandora's Daughters: The Role and Status of Women in Greek and Roman Antiquity*, Johns Hopkins, 1987; Jane F. Gardner, *Women in Roman Law and Society*, Croom Helm, 1986 (Indiana Univ. Press, 1986); Sarah B. Pomeroy, *Goddesses, Whores, Wives and Slaves: Women in Classical Antiquity*, Schocken Books, 1975.

# PATUM
# PEPERIUM

Why can't women be Church of England priests? An Anglican curate, interviewed in the *Independent*, 'said that you might as well ordain a pot of anchovy paste as a woman. The action is physically possible in both cases; in neither did he believe it would be efficacious.'[1]

Anchovy paste, patum peperium, gentleman's relish; it comes in elegant pots proclaiming 'original 1828 recipe' and bearing the legend 'use sparingly'. The curate is, we are told, a 'camp Anglo-Catholic'; what he meant to insinuate by using the comparison was, presumably, that women are constitutionally lacking in some vital ingredient without which it is impossible to become a priest. The attraction of the priesthood for some men may well be the unparalleled opportunity it offers for wearing dresses, but why pick on anchovy paste? The sexual imagery is irresistible: the paste is made of fish, a smell strongly and pejoratively associated with the female genitals; it is famously spicy and strong, for use only in small quantities; it is traditionally served in gentlemen's clubs, institutions in which men gather with the object of spending time away from women. Sexual disgust, fear of female sexuality, a desire for sexual apartheid: our clever curate has boiled down thousands of years of hostility to women into one telling phrase.

Judaeo-Christian men have always had trouble coping with women. In Orthodox Jewish ritual, men have traditionally been required to start the day by giving thanks for not being made a woman. According to the author of Ecclesiasticus, 'All wickedness is but little to the wickedness of a woman.'[2] In Ecclesiastes we read: 'The wiles of a woman I find mightier than death; her heart is a trap to catch you and her arms are fetters.'[3] St Paul said: 'It is a good thing for a man to have nothing to do with women.'[4] He also remarked that women must not address meetings; if they wanted to know something, they should ask their husbands at home.[5] The theologian Tertullian, writing at the beginning of the third century AD, remarked: 'How much better a man feels when he happens to be away from his wife.'[6] St Augustine, writing in the late fourth and early fifth centuries, said: 'What is the difference whether it is in a wife or in a mother, it is still Eve the temptress that we must beware of in any woman.'[7] Few have gone quite as far as Odo of Cluny (AD 879–942), who opined that: 'To embrace a woman is to embrace a sack of manure.'[8] For St Thomas Aquinas, a hugely influential writer of the thirteenth century, woman was merely 'defective and misbegotten'.[9] But even Richard Rolle, a fourteenth-century English hermit whose book *The Fire of Love* reveals a refreshingly cheerful cast of mind and who was once rebuked by a lady of his acquaintance for admiring her 'great bosom', concluded: 'Be wise, then, and flee from women.'[10]

The specific question of women priests in the Anglican Church has drawn reactions of scorn and dismay ever since Dr Johnson dismissed them thus in 1763: 'A woman's preaching is like a dog's walking on his hinder legs. It is not done well; but you are surprised to find it done at all.'[11] In recent years, as the issue has threatened to split the Church of England, the debate has been characterized by the emotional rather than intellectual tone of the opposition. For Peregrine Worsthorne, editor of the *Sunday Telegraph*, the ordination of women would turn attendance at church from a 'cosy, familiar experience' into 'a stressful challenge; a journey into unknown territory'.[12] In a burst of chauvinism notable for its apparent ignorance of British monarchical history, he adds that most English people 'would no more welcome a woman at the altar than they would a foreigner on the throne'. His article ends with an exhortation which might have come from the mouth of any Christian theologian in the last two thousand years: 'But spare us, oh Lord, the female of the species.' Another vocal opponent of women priests, the Tory MP and junior government minister John Selwyn Gummer, said in 1987 that he would leave the Church if it ordained women priests. 'It would no longer be the Church into which I was born, which I love and in which I hope to die,'[13] he moaned. His then parliamentary colleague, the voluble Peter Bruinvels, described the slow progress towards reform of Synod, the Church's governing body, as 'a disaster'.[14] He warned of 'no-go areas' for women priests and issued this rallying call: 'I call on all Anglicans throughout the land to fight this legislation from within and only to join a Church of England in exile if we lose.'

The job of articulating the case, such as it is, against women priests has fallen to Dr Graham Leonard, the Bishop of London. His arguments seem to fall into two categories, those of biology and theology. He rehearsed the first in an interview with John Mortimer in the *Sunday Times* in 1985.[15] Asked why Mrs Thatcher, for example, would not make a good bishop, he replied:

> That's an excellent question and I'll give you an answer which has nothing whatever to do with whether or not you think Mrs Thatcher is a good prime minister. It comes down to the biological difference between men

and women, why women aren't the right people to be priests.

This is obvious nonsense; the most glaring biological difference between a man and a woman, the possession of a penis and testicles by the former and a vagina and breasts by the latter, can have no possible bearing on how either carries out the duties of a priest. A little later in the interview, Leonard provides a gloss on his assertion: 'Biologically man takes the initiative. Woman receives and is feminine.' Such stuff would hardly pass muster in a GCSE exam, but then Leonard is not the first person to confuse the feminine with the female (and, by extension, the masculine with the male). A vast body of research into the supposed difference between the sexes above and beyond the reproductive function has come up with really very little apart from the male's generally superior physical strength and minor disparities in the ability to tackle Mensa-type puzzles, neither of which has much obvious relevance to the priestly vocation. Most of the other differences attributed to biology, far from being innate, have to be taught; that is why little girls are dressed in pink and given dolls while boys wear blue and play with guns. It is tempting to ask why, if Leonard is convinced that there are biological reasons which prevent women from doing the job of priests, he is so anxious to prevent their being given the chance to prove him triumphantly right.

The bishop does little better when it comes to theology. He is out of step with opinion in the Church of England; as long ago as 1965 the General Synod voted that 'there are no fundamental objections to the ordination of women to the priesthood'. His argument, as he explained it to John Mortimer, is this:

It's not an accident that when God became 'man' He chose to be a male. There's no doubt that He could have chosen to be a woman if He'd wanted to.[16]

In an interview in 1988, with Andrew Brown of the *Independent*,[17] Leonard put it another way: 'He [God] chose a patriarchal society. It wasn't an accidental time.' The obvious objection to this line of reasoning is that it is hard to identify many points in history when God could have become incarnate in anything but a patriarchal society.

Some opponents of female ordination rest their case on quotations from the Bible. Their objections carry little more weight than those of Leonard, since their choice of material is highly selective. The Bible forbids many things, including lending money at interest ('usury') and divorce (St Paul says: 'To the married I give this ruling, which is not mine but the Lord's: a wife must not separate herself from her husband; if she does, she must either remain unmarried or be reconciled to her husband; and the husband must not divorce his wife'[18]), to which the Church of England now takes a more relaxed attitude. But they do at least provide a pointer to the origins of the sexual disgust and fear of women which have been a hallmark of the Christian Church for centuries and which are the secret, if unconscious, motivation of those who oppose the ordination of women.

St Augustine, in the passage quoted earlier, warned men to beware of 'Eve the temptress' in every woman; we learn right at the beginning of the Bible, in Genesis, that it was Eve who was responsible for the fall. She was created from Adam's rib, to be his companion, but initially there is nothing sexual about their relationship: 'Now they were both naked, the man and his wife, but they had no feeling of shame towards one another.'[19]

The serpent, recognizing Eve as the weaker vessel, tempts her with knowledge. She eats first, then offers the fruit to Adam. The immediate result is the discovery of sexual difference, and the shame that goes with it: 'Then the eyes of both of them were opened and they discovered that they were naked; so they stitched fig-leaves together and made themselves loincloths.'[20] Something is lacking, however, and that is desire. It is not until God appears in the garden to punish both man and woman that this element enters the story, and it does so specifically as God's *punishment* for Eve. To her he says:

> I will increase your labour and your groaning,
> and in labour you shall bear children.
> You shall be eager for your husband,
> and he shall be your master.[21]

Adam also has to pay a penalty; he must work the thorny ground to scrape together food, and eventually he will die. The punishment is meted out first because 'you have listened to your wife'[22] and only second because he has eaten from the forbidden tree. The logic of the story is inescapable: the whole thing is Eve's fault; her sentence is sexual desire which is the instrument through which she will be subjugated to her husband and feel the pain of childbirth. He, on the other hand, is punished with unremitting work and eventual death, constant reminders of his folly in trusting a woman.

These ideas—woman as the source of danger for man, woman as the repository of lust—had a powerful effect on the early Church. In the third century AD, Tertullian wrote a treatise

called *De cultu feminarum* — 'On Female Dress' — in which he said
that every woman should dress 'as Eve mourning and repentant'
in order to expiate 'that which she derives from Eve — the igno-
miny, I mean, of the first sin, and the odium of human perdi-
tion'.[23] He went on:

> And do you not know that you are an Eve? The sentence
> of God on this sex of yours lives in this age: the guilt
> must of necessity live too. *You* are the devil's gateway:
> *you* are the unsealer of that tree: *you* are the first deserter
> of the divine law: *you* are she who persuaded him whom
> the devil was not valiant enough to attack. *You* destroyed
> so easily God's image, man. On account of *your* desert—
> that is, death—even the Son of God had to die.

Of course, Tertullian's ban on wearing pretty clothes, jewellery and hair dye was not based solely on his belief that every
woman must pay for the sin of Eve. His hatred of women was
equalled by his hatred of sex (the two things frequently go hand
in hand) and he was anxious that Christians do everything they
could to avoid inspiring or feeling lust. In his *Exhortation to
Chastity*, written between AD 204 and 212, he wrote:

> But then, it is objected, is not your doctrine destructive
> of all marriage, even monogamy?—Yes, and with good
> reason, since this, too, in the shameful act which consti-
> tutes its essence, is the same as fornication.[24]

St Jerome, who was born in or near the year 342, a couple
of hundred years later than Tertullian, was deeply horrified by
the idea of sex, as he revealed in a letter to a Christian widow
who sought his advice as to whether she should marry again (the

final sentence is a famous quote from the Second Letter of Peter in the New Testament):

> The trials of marriage you have learned in the married state: you have been surfeited to nausea as though with the flesh of quails. Your mouth has tasted the bitterest of gall, you have voided the sour unwholesome food, you have relieved a heaving stomach. Why would you put into it again something which has already proved harmful to you?[25] *The dog is turned to his own vomit again and the sow that was washed to her wallowing in the mire.*

Richard Rolle, in the fourteenth century, did not share Jerome's loathing of sex but was still worried by women's tendency—like Eve—to lead men into sin, even if he expressed himself in more temperate language than Tertullian:

> But friendship between men and women can be a tricky business because a pretty face all too easily attracts a weak soul, and visual temptation kindles carnal lust, often to produce a defiled mind and body. Familiarity between men and women is apt to turn to virtue's disadvantage.[26]

But it would be wrong to assume from Rolle's lack of stridency that the story of the fall was weakening its baleful grip on the minds of Christians with the passing of the centuries. Around the same time, in a development which was to be responsible for the massacre of thousands of women in Northern Europe, woman-as-Eve was being transformed into woman-as-witch; as a result the Church, in the shape of the Inquisition, was able to torture, drown, hang and burn those women who did not match the narrow Christian ideal of womanhood. Although the

Inquisition did not operate in England, the Church's warnings about witchcraft still had a powerful grip on people's imaginations: Alice Perrers, the mistress of Edward III, was accused of ensnaring the King through magic, and her doctor was arrested and charged with preparing love potions on her behalf; Joan of Navarre, stepmother of Henry V, was accused of using witchcraft in an attempt to kill him. The function of examining witches in England was enthusiastically appropriated by the state; in one of the most famous cases, that of the Pendle witches, eight women and two men were sentenced to hang in 1612 after a trial at Lancaster Castle.

In 1484, Pope Innocent VIII became anxious about an outbreak of witchcraft which was said to have taken place in Northern Germany. He appointed two Dominican monks, Heinrich Kramer and James Sprenger, both members of the Inquisition, to investigate and stamp it out. The two men produced a massive account of their work—the translation runs to over 500 pages—which amounts to nothing less than a handbook for witch-hunters. The *Malleus Maleficarum* ('The Hammer of Witches')[27] was probably first published in 1486 and received the approval of the Church in the shape of an endorsement from the Faculty of Theology of the University of Cologne a year later. It was immediately popular, running to fourteen editions between 1487 and 1520, and at least sixteen between 1574 and 1669.

What emerges above all else from this extraordinary document is the Church's pathological loathing of women. Kramer and Sprenger detested them, rewriting history and myth to fit in with their view of women's overweening and malicious influence on the world. In an important early section of the *Malleus* they write:

If we inquire, we find that nearly all the kingdoms of the world have been overthrown by women. Troy, which was a prosperous kingdom, was, for the rape of one woman, Helen, destroyed, and many thousands of Greeks slain. The kingdom of the Jews suffered much misfortune and destruction through the accursed Jezebel, and her daughter Athaliah, queen of Judah, who caused her son's sons to be killed, that on their death she might reign herself; yet each of them was slain. The kingdom of the Romans endured much evil through Cleopatra, Queen of Egypt, that worst of women. And so with others. Therefore it is no wonder that the world now suffers through the malice of women.[28]

Helen is blamed for the fall of Troy even though, according to this version of the story—which is not the usual one—she was the victim of rape. The authors are also rather hard on Cleopatra, who played a relatively minor role in the turbulent events that brought about the end of the Roman republic. But this is the *Malleus* view of history: woman, specifically sexually active woman, is the most powerfully destructive force in the world. In a key passage, Kramer and Sprenger go on to explain why:

And now let us examine the carnal desires of the body itself, whence has arisen unconscionable harm to human life. Justly may we say with Cato of Utica: If the world could be rid of women, we should not be without God in our intercourse. For truly, without the wickedness of women, to say nothing of witchcraft, the world would remain proof against innumerable dangers. Hear what Valerius said to Rufinus: You do not know that woman is the Chimaera, but it is good that you should know it; for that monster was of three forms; its face was that of a radiant and noble lion, it had the filthy belly of a goat,

and it was armed with the virulent tail of a viper. And
he means that a woman is beautiful to look upon, con-
taminating to the touch, and deadly to keep.[29]

Here an idea from Genesis is being taken even further:
woman is now not only the repository of lust but *its instigator
in men*. In other words, whenever a man and a woman engage
in sex, consensually or not, regardless of the circumstances, it is
the woman's fault—it is always she who causes it to happen.
When it comes to sex, *men are not to blame*; a world without
women would be a world without desire. Kramer and Sprenger
make clear that this propensity on the part of women towards lust
is caused by a fault in their make-up; women are *biologically*
different from men (shades of Graham Leonard):

> For as regards intellect, or the understanding of spiritual
> things, they seem to be of a different nature from men;
> a fact which is vouched for by the logic of the authori-
> ties, backed by various examples from the Scriptures.
> Terence says: Women are intellectually like chil-
> dren . . .
>
> But the natural reason [why a woman is intellectu-
> ally inferior] is that she is more carnal than a man, as is
> clear from her many carnal abominations. And it should
> be noted that there was a defect in the formation of the
> first woman, since she was formed from a bent rib, that
> is, rib of the breast, which is bent as it were in a contrary
> direction to a man. And since through this defect she is
> an imperfect animal, she always deceives.[30]

This passage is taken from a chapter of the *Malleus* in which
the authors discuss why superstition—by which they mean a

weakness for witchcraft—'is chiefly found in Women'. The reason is simple: 'All witchcraft comes from carnal lust, which is in women insatiable.'[31] Indeed, it is often the case that the reason why men feel desire—or fail to feel it—is that they have been bewitched, and the *Malleus* gives examples:

> And there was in the town of Mersburg in the diocese of Constance a certain young man who was bewitched in such a way that he could never perform the carnal act with any woman except one. And many have heard him tell that he had often wished to refuse that woman, and take flight to other lands; but that hitherto he had been compelled to rise up in the night and to come very quickly back, sometimes over land, and sometimes through the air as if he were flying.[32]

It is not a big step from locating women as the instigator of desire in both sexes to believing that they therefore control it—and have the power to take it away. A whole chapter of the *Malleus* is entitled 'How, as it were, they Deprive Man of his Virile Member,' and consists of a series of fantasies in which witches cause men to suffer loss of the penis. It is ironic, of course, that the part of the male body which most symbolizes masculine power—the penis and testicles—should, because of its exposed position, be relatively vulnerable, at once the source of power and weakness. For the authors of the *Malleus*, it is natural that witches should seek to assert their authority over men by attacking them in this area; we are in the familiar territory of the castrating bitch/witch. The book reports the experience of a Dominican monk who was approached by a young man who claimed that 'he had lost his member'.[33] The monk requested the young man to remove his clothes, inspected his body, and confirmed his claim. Then he asked 'whether he suspected anyone of having so bewitched him'. The youth's reply was in the affirmative, and the monk advised him to 'go to her as soon as possible and try your utmost to soften her with gentle words and promises'. A few days later the young man returned with his penis back in place.

The authors of the *Malleus* do not, they point out at some length, actually believe that witches have the power to remove the penis from the body; they simply cast a spell to conceal it. But women's power to create illusion, and that of the devils with whom they are in league, is enormous, as is shown by the following story. The authors report that witches have been known to 'collect male organs in great numbers, as many as twenty or thirty members together, and put them in a bird's nest'.[34] They tell the story of a man who, having lost his penis, approached a witch in the hope of having it restored:

> She told the afflicted man to climb a certain tree, and that he might take which he liked out of a nest in which there were several members. And when he tried to take a big one, the witch said: You must not take that one; adding, because it belonged to a parish priest.[35]

The final detail is interesting; the witch is supposed to be mocking the Church by imputing unusual sexual potency to one of its priests (who should be celibate), but the familiar obsession with the size of the penis suggests that the story is a male invention. But then the *Malleus* is a very masculine document, a fantasy about the evil nature of female sexuality created from myth, stories from the Bible, and hearsay in order to justify the Church's persecution of insubordinate women. It is important to bear in mind when examining these ideas that Kramer and Sprenger were not mavericks, that the *Malleus* was written at the behest of the Church and received the blessing of prominent theologians; for them, each woman who burned was a guilty daughter of Eve. They seem to have overlooked the point that, according to their own cosmology, women were doomed by their very nature to follow her example; if anatomy really is destiny, is it fair to punish those who cannot help themselves? This question appears not to have troubled the minds of the Inquisition: they went about their task with gusto, behaving as though every woman, weak as she might be, had a duty to overcome the desires of the flesh and model herself on the Blessed Virgin Mary.

Ah yes, Mary. The Virgin is a hugely significant Christian image; it is she whom Christian men cite when, against the evidence of the centuries, they need to defend the Church against the charge of woman-hating. Has she not, they ask, been accorded the highest honours—almost, in the Roman Catholic faith, to the point of idolatry? But putting women on pedestals is one of those devious masculine devices whose meaning is exactly the opposite of what it appears to be. Far from constituting a celebration of female power—where this one woman is concerned, at any rate—it is a way of denying it: the woman we have honoured in this way is *good*, which is to say that her behaviour falls within acceptable parameters, and therefore she does not pose a threat to us; we do not need to worry about her. In any case Mary is, it has to be said, a pretty hopeless role model for other women; it is impossible for any of us to copy her. Both Catholicism and the Church of England adhere to the doctrine of the virgin birth and Mary's perpetual virginity thereafter, denying sex its natural function even within marriage. A state of married celibacy appeals to few women, and not even nuns are able to replicate

Mary's extraordinary feat of sex-free maternity. It is all of a piece; the story of Christ's birth, far from elevating the status of the female sex, is simply further proof that Christianity was conceived in sexual disgust and loathing of women, setting a standard against which all must fall. *Of course* the traditionalists of the Church of England reject the notion of women priests; every woman is Eve, but none of us will ever be another Mary.

1 *Independent*, 23 February 1987.
2 Ecclesiasticus 25:19.
3 Ecclesiastes 7:26.
4 1 Corinthians 7:1.
5 1 Corinthians 14:34–5.
6 Tertullian, *An Exhortation To Chastity (De exhortatione castitatis)*, translated by William P. Le Saint in *Tertullian, Treatises on Marriage and Remarriage*, The Newman Press, 1951, p. 58.
7 Augustine, Letter 243:10, quoted in Karen Armstrong, *The Gospel According to Woman*, Pan, 1986, p. 61 (Doubleday, 1987).
8 Quoted ibid., p. 23.
9 Thomas Aquinas, *Summa theologica IV*, Part I, Quaest XCII, art. 1, quoted ibid., p. 62.
10 Richard Rolle, *The Fire of Love*, translated into modern English by Clifton Wolters, Penguin, 1972, p. 136.
11 *The Oxford Dictionary of Quotations*, OUP, 1979. p. 275, No. 10.
12 *Sunday Telegraph*, 22 February 1987.
13 *Daily Telegraph*, 27 February 1987.
14 Ibid.
15 *Sunday Times*, 22 December 1985.
16 Ibid.
17 *Independent*, 12 April 1988.
18 1 Corinthians 7:10–11.
19 Genesis 2:25.
20 Genesis 3:7.
21 Genesis 3:16.
22 Genesis 3:17–19.

23  All quotations from *On Female Dress (De cultu feminarum)*, Tertullian, *Writings*, Vol. 1 (from the Ante-Nicene Christian Library Series), T. and T. Clark, Edinburgh, 1869, pp. 304–5.

24  William P. Le Saint, op. cit., p. 57.

25  Jerome, *Letters*, quoted in Armstrong, op. cit., p. 60.

26  Richard Rolle, op. cit., p. 175.

27  All quotations from *Malleus Maleficarum: The Classic Study of Witchcraft*, translated by Montague Summers, Arrow Books, 1971 (Dover, 1971).

28  Ibid., pp. 120–1.

29  Ibid., p. 121.

30  Ibid., pp. 116–7.

31  Ibid., p. 122.

32  Ibid., p. 262.

33  Ibid., pp. 263–4.

34  Ibid., pp. 267–8.

35  Ibid., p. 268.

# WOMEN IN TOGAS

Was ancient Rome an empire without women? So it would seem, from a glance at some of the books written about the city. Here is the opening passage of *The Romans*, an ambitiously titled volume published by Pelican in 1949 as part of its popular history series:

> What manner of men were the Romans? We commonly say that men are known best by their deeds; therefore to answer this question it would be wise to go, first, to Roman history for the deeds, and secondly, to Roman literature for the mind behind the deeds.[1]

The argument usually put forward in defence of this manner of writing is that the word 'man' should be read to include both sexes in certain contexts. But in sentence after sentence the author, R. H. Barrow, makes it clear that his vision of Rome is peopled only by men:

> The Roman loved his country, and he loved to possess land and to take up the challenge which it offered. He took from it the joy of ownership and the satisfaction of making it produce.[2]

Given the state of Roman property law for most of the city's history, this joyful band of farmers and land-owners is hardly

likely to include many women. A clue to the reason behind
Barrow's assumption that the Romans were men can be found
in this observation about their literature:

> On the highest plane the actions of men are the subject-
> matter of epic. To the Roman, epic is, of course, the epic
> of Rome; Rome is the heroine inspiring Romans to
> heroic deeds to fulfil her destiny.[3]

Metaphorical females are easier to deal with than the real
thing, as Aeneas implicitly recognized when he left Dido to death
and disgrace in Carthage and set off for Italy to found the eternal
city. At any rate, R. H. Barrow certainly had tradition on his side
in the matter of gender-specific historical vision. Thomas Godwyn, who wrote *An English Exposition of the Romane Antiquities*
for the boys of Abingdon School in 1623, similarly confined
himself to the exploits of half the Roman empire. His book
includes a great deal of information on everything from who was
allowed to wear gold rings (men of senatorial rank) to methods
of capturing a foreign city with siege engines, but precious little
about the lives of Roman women. The book conveys the impression that this omission sits happily with Godwyn's wider view
of the world, his conviction that women should know their place;
one of his rare references to the female sex is to inveigh against
Roman women who dared appropriate for themselves that exclusively male form of dress, the toga. No decent woman, no woman
'of any credit', would do such a thing; so disgraceful was this
behaviour, he says, that the 'old Poets, when they would point
out unto us an infamous or lewde strumpet, they would tearme
her *Mulierem togatam*'.[4]

Although the phrase translates literally as 'a woman dressed
in a toga', its tone is comparable to the disparaging English saying

about a bossy woman—that she is 'the one who wears the trousers' in such and such a house or marriage. With Roman history in the hands of men like Barrow and Godwyn, it is hardly surprising that the females who do get a passing mention in traditional accounts of Rome are a drab and submissive lot, walk-on parts in a majestic cavalcade of kings, consuls and emperors; they stand well behind their menfolk, and their faces are in shadow. Here, close to the front of the procession, is Lucretia, possibly the world's most famous rape victim (she died by her own hand, and thus preserved her husband's good name). Next comes Claudia, an early adherent of the feminine mystique; her gratified spouse recorded her achievements on her tombstone as *lanam fecit, domum servit* [5]—she wove wool and kept the house. The next woman is dwarfed by a crowd of famous men, including her father, the celebrated general Scipio Africanus. Her name is Cornelia, a mother of twelve famous for her refusal to wear precious gems: 'These are my jewels,'[6] she protests, counting the children who flock about her.

Isn't there something odd about this? Rome is famous for its lyric poetry, and these exemplary housewives and mothers seem unlikely muses to have inspired love poems whose passion blazes to the present day. Surely there were women who kicked against the restraints, who wanted more than arranged marriages and the narrow lot of the Roman matron? There were. Gaius Valerius Catullus, foremost among the Roman lyric poets, addressed his most passionate poems to a woman he disguised with the pseudonym Lesbia, a woman who inspired him to extremes of love and hate. What was *she* like?

She is believed to have been a woman called Clodia, wife of a man named Metellus who governed Northern Italy in 63 BC. We find a brief description of her by the academic Robert

Rowland in his introduction to a translation of Catullus's poems
by James Michie:

> An aristocratic woman with an eminent but dull and
> pompous husband, Clodia was several years older than
> Catullus. The identification [of Clodia with Lesbia],
> questioned by a few scholars, seems certain. In any case,
> it does not matter who Clodia was; what matters is that
> Catullus loved her and eventually, after a long and pain-
> ful struggle with himself, broke away from her spell.[7]

The tradition is maintained: Clodia is dismissed in a few
words, with the emphasis once again on Roman *men*. Fortunately, other classicists have had more to say on the subject of
Clodia. One of them is the distinguished scholar Gilbert Highet,
a former Oxford don who later became Professor of Greek and
Latin at Columbia University. His famous book on Roman
writers and their background, *Poets in a Landscape*, first published
in 1957, has a whole chapter on Catullus and includes a great deal
of information about the poet's girlfriend. It begins with a concise introductory sketch of the life and significance of Catullus.
The poet came from the north of Italy, lived 'a brief, passionate,
unhappy life', and introduced a new word for kiss—*basium*—
into the European languages to amuse his lover. Highet concludes: 'The woman was unworthy. The poet died. The word
lives.'[8]

A few pages into the chapter we learn that Clodia was 'a
really formidable woman'. She was beautiful, with striking eyes;
she danced 'exquisitely'; she adored poetry. But she is said to have
indulged in 'a little incest' with her younger brother, Publius
Clodius, and her husband, according to Highet, died 'with suspi-

cious abruptness'. His death marked her release: 'She could do virtually anything she wanted; and she did.'[9]

It is already clear that Highet does not like Clodia; equally, it is obvious that she had little in common with the Roman matrons admired by historians. It is not long before the reason for his hostility manifests itself:

> Her life ended not in despair, but in derision. She did not mind degrading herself to any depth in order to get attention and excitement. From her garden, she could watch the young men swimming in the Tiber, and signal to them. She would sleep with a grinning Spaniard— who, says Catullus, kept his teeth brilliant by polishing them with his own urine. She would pick up strangers in vile taverns and in filthy back streets.[10]

Highet's comments on Clodia are motivated by sexual disgust, and the basest sort of disgust at that; these are not *facts* about Clodia, disinterestedly recorded by contemporary sources, but insults hurled at her by a jealous lover at times when their stormy relationship had broken down. The Clodia who emerges from some of the poems is a cruel and capricious tease, an unfaithful and unfeeling whore, but any sensible reader can see that the picture they paint is coloured by strong emotion. Highet's gloss on one particular phrase used by Catullus gives him away; referring to the words *identidem omnium ilia rumpens*[11]—which mean that she exhausted her lovers, that she 'broke their balls', to employ a modern metaphor—he observes:

> She uses them up, and, instead of invigorating them as a truly loving woman would, destroys their manhood in satisfying herself.[12]

There is nothing like a sexually active, orgasmic woman to strike fear into the heart of a conservative male academic; the prudishness and disgust with which Highet responds to Clodia, and which lead him to believe the worst of her, is part of a tradition which does much to explain how Cambridge dons came to observe a rule forbidding marriage right up until 1878 (female dons were admitted even later). But what is really inexcusable in a supposedly rigorous academic intellect is the disingenuousness with which Highet handles his sources. There is abundant evidence that the affair between Clodia and Catullus was both passionate and unstable, punctuated by frequent break-ups and reconciliations, and it is not clear whether it had been completely broken off before the poet's untimely death, probably around the year 54 BC, in his early thirties. The most bitter of the poems, in which he rails against Clodia's infidelity and lists the men she is supposed to have taken as lovers in his place, were obviously written at times of intolerable emotional stress. They are terrific poems, but they hardly establish Catullus as a reliable witness— relying on his word is rather like asking Othello what he thinks of Desdemona halfway through Act Five. Perhaps Highet was sensitive to the impeachability of his source; at any rate, he makes much of the fact that there is another contemporary account of Clodia, one which also shows her in a very poor light.

The author of this account, according to Highet, is 'the greatest speaker of his time or of any other time',[13] the orator Cicero. This alone should be enough to set alarm bells ringing; Cicero was a tiresome old moralist, a pompous *nouveau riche* who continually harked back to a romanticized version of the past when women were content to fill their days with domestic duties. Highet's version of the story is that Cicero sprang to the defence of a man called Caelius, a young politician, when Clodia brought false charges against him; her motive, according to Highet, was a desire for revenge after Caelius abandoned her:

> When Caelius Rufus left her, she prosecuted him for attempting to poison her.
>
> The charge was ridiculous. (She added others, equally ridiculous.) The evidence was flimsy. Clodia did not know what moderation was.[14]

Highet's dismissal of the prosecution case is puzzling, the speeches outlining it having been lost. What we do have is a famous slur on Clodia included by Caelius in his speech in his own defence—that she was *in triclinio Coa, in cubiculo Noa*[15] (eager in the dining-room, frigid in the bedroom)—and Cicero's courtroom diatribe against her. This latter takes the form of a lengthy piece of character assassination designed to show that Clodia, in spite of her society connections, was to all intents and purposes a prostitute—a class of person whose evidence carried next to no weight in a Roman court, if it was admitted at all. The speech was a triumph; Caelius was acquitted, and Clodia was shown up, in Highet's words, as 'a vile trollop, a cross between a clown and a whore'.[16] This picture of her, embellished by the jealous gibes of Catullus, is what has come down to us.

Yet Cicero is no more impartial a witness than Catullus. He and Clodia were far from strangers to each other before their encounter in court. Clodia's brother, Publius Clodius, was Cicero's bitterest enemy. The two men were on opposite sides in the internecine power struggle which was about to engulf the Roman republic and lead to the establishment of the empire. A few years before, Clodius had instigated a legal action which led to Cicero's temporary banishment from Rome; the orator's house in the city was destroyed during his enforced absence, and that of his brother was set on fire. The hostility between the two men can be measured by the fact that when Clodius was killed in a street ambush four years after the trial of Caelius, Cicero defended the man accused of his murder. When Cicero set out publicly to demolish Clodia's character, his chief motivation was a spiteful desire to attack Clodius through his sister.

As sources on Clodia, Cicero and Catullus are equally tainted. Two thousand years later, it is difficult to judge what she was really like. Yet the information we have about her, slanted as it is, is sufficient to establish that she was educated, attractive and independent—a creature of an entirely different cast from the Lucretias and Cornelias who were held up as examples for Roman matrons to follow. Nor, it seems, was she unique. Gilbert Highet's book has chapters on several other Roman poets, among them Tibullus and Propertius. By an astonishing coincidence, they too had promiscuous, unfaithful girlfriends. This is how Highet sums up Tibullus:

> He was passionately devoted to at least two mistresses: Plania (whom he disguised in the poetic manner as 'Delia'), and a woman with the sinister name of Nemesis. The second was a greedy, conscienceless creature who loved nothing but herself and cash. The first was not much better. Yet what is most striking in his life is his almost entire subservience to them. Rich, handsome, talented as he was, with the world at his feet, he preferred to be dominated by two tramps.[17]

Tibullus was probably born in or around 55 BC. Propertius was born four or five years later. His lover, Hostia, whom he called Cynthia in his poems, was well-born, beautiful and educated; it seems that she even wrote poems. Over to Highet:

She was hard and cruel to Propertius—almost as hard as Clodia had been to Catullus, but with less sordid vulgarity, with a good deal more style and dash, and with something much more like real love in the intervals of anger, doubt, and infidelity.[18]

Highet then goes on to concede that the infidelity was not all on one side (Propertius himself admits as much in one of the poems). He continues:

If Propertius and Cynthia had had less talent, less money, less of a passion for independence, less of the disease of irresponsibility that was spreading through Rome like an epidemic, they might well have married, and lived an irregular but stimulating life. But marriage, with its obligations and its staid manners and regular routine, revolted them.[19]

'The disease of irresponsibility'; Highet is beginning to sound like a right-wing columnist, Paul Johnson say, inveighing against the permissiveness of the 1960s in the *Spectator*. The analogy is not inapt, and leads us to the heart of the mystery, which is why Highet should feel such palpable disgust for these spirited and unusual women who inspired some of the world's greatest love poetry.

The answer is that he has unquestioningly absorbed the conventional wisdom of two thousand years of woman-hating. The tradition owes its foundations not simply to Victorian academics or early Christian commentators but to the Romans themselves. For a period of two or three hundred years stretching very roughly from 100 BC, Roman women of certain classes enjoyed an incomparable freedom of movement. That freedom, exploited to the hilt by Clodia, Cynthia, and others whose names we do not know, was as much a blow to Rome's stern and unbending moralists as would have been the children of the 1960s who declared themselves in favour of free love and against everything their parents had brought them up to believe in. In Rome, as in England and the United States two thousand years later, the reaction was both immediate and horrified; as soon as women began finding ways round the property laws which gave them effective control of money, as soon as they took advantage of an increasing body of knowledge about contraception and abortion to free themselves from constant child-bearing, Roman men began to complain. Nor were they slow to translate words into action; the emperor Augustus, horrified by the dramatic fall in the birth rate among upper-class women, adopted the stick-and-carrot approach by passing laws which made it illegal for adults not to marry, and by giving tax advantages to large families. To no avail; women carried on taking lovers and limiting their families, and writers like Juvenal were driven to paroxysms of fury by their intractability and forward behaviour. Roman litera-ture is peppered with attacks on female morals and mores, none more intemperate and sustained than Juvenal's famous Sixth Sat-ire, a poem of over 600 lines which is a paean to woman-hating and sexual disgust.

It begins, appropriately enough, with oblique references to Clodia and Cynthia who, though long dead (Juvenal published the poem around AD 115–17), continued to exercise the minds of Roman men as reminders of when things had begun to go wrong. (The Penguin translation of the satire is by Peter Green, an English academic who emigrated to the US and became Professor of Classics at the University of Texas at Austin. Green's attitude to Cynthia and Clodia is not dissimilar to Highet's; he describes them in a note as 'neurotic, sophisticated creatures with the

loosest of sexual habits'.[20]) Having established his subject, Juvenal
quickly gets into his stride, warning his friend Postumus that it
would be better to commit suicide or sleep with a boy than
commit the folly of matrimony:

> Boys don't quarrel all night, or nag you for little presents
> While they're on the job, or complain that you don't come
> Up to their expectations, or demand more gasping passion.[21]

He claims that Roman women have become so sex-mad that
they'll sleep with anyone, a flute-player or a guitarist whose child
will then be passed off as their legitimate offspring. Some women
don't want children at all, enjoying themselves with eunuchs to
avoid abortions; for others, 'our skilled abortionists know all the
answers'.[22] A fascinating picture of freedom and independence
emerges as Juvenal complains about Roman women taking danc-
ing and music lessons:

> Yet a musical wife's not so bad as some presumptuous
> Flat-chested busybody who rushes around the town
> Gate-crashing all-male meetings, talking back straight-faced
> To a uniformed general—*and* in her husband's presence.[23]

Every age carries with it a notion of the ideal woman; the
Roman version, with its emphasis on chastity, submissiveness and
homely virtues, is not so very different from that of the clerics
and male dons who made the city's literature their private province until very recently indeed. Clodia, Plania, and Hostia have
suffered at their hands for two thousand years, erased from their
rightful place in history or viewed through a lens of thick,
distorting glass which has turned them into caricatures. W. B.
Yeats once reflected that the real Catullus would terrify the aged

academics—the 'old, learned, respectable bald heads'[24]—who had spent years of their lives trying to understand him. It is not difficult to imagine the stampede that would take place if not Catullus but Clodia suddenly appeared in their midst and settled herself into a seat at High Table.

1 R. H. Barrow, *The Romans*, Pelican, 1949, p. 9.

2 Ibid., pp. 130–1.

3 Ibid., p. 117.

4 Thomas Godwyn, *Romanae historiae anthologia recognita et aucta* ('An English Exposition of the Romane Antiquities'), printed by John Lichfield and James Short for Henry Crypps, Oxford, 1623, p. 150.

5 Quoted in Eva Cantarella, *Pandora's Daughters: The Role and Status of Women in Greek and Roman Antiquity*, Johns Hopkins, 1987, p. 133.

6 Ibid., p. 130.

7 *The Poems of Catullus*, translated by James Michie, Panther, 1972, pp. 10–11.

8 Gilbert Highet, *Poets in a Landscape*, Pelican, 1959, p. 17.

9 Ibid., p. 25.

10 Ibid., p. 45.

11 Catullus, Poem 11.

12 Highet, op. cit., p. 37.

13 Ibid., p. 46.

14 Ibid., p. 45.

15 Recorded by Quintilian; quoted in T. P. Wiseman, *Catullus and his World*, Cambridge University Press, 1985, p. 76.

16 Highet, op. cit., p. 49.

17 Ibid., p. 162.

18 Ibid., p. 90.

19 Ibid., p. 90.

20 Juvenal, *The Sixteen Satires*, translated by Peter Green, Penguin, 1974, p. 153.

21 Ibid., p. 128.

22 Ibid., p. 149.

23 Ibid., p. 142.

24 W. B. Yeats, 'The Scholars', *Collected Poems*, Macmillan, 1961, p. 158.

# MEN ONLY

Imagine a society in which women are kept secluded in their own part of the house, forbidden to go out even to do the shopping, permitted to mix with strangers only at ceremonial occasions like funerals. The Ayatollah's Iran? Pakistan under General Zia? No, we are talking about the cradle of democracy, Athens in the fifth century BC. This is how Eva Cantarella, Professor of Roman Law at the University of Parma, describes the everyday lives of women during this vitally important period of history:

> Closed off in the internal part of the house to which the men did not have access, the married woman had no chance to meet persons other than members of the household. In Athens, men even did the shopping. Wives (and, for that matter, mothers, sisters, and daughters) could not attend banquets.[1]

There is nothing unusual about this, given that most of history is the history of patriarchy—although it is the case that women in the militaristic and authoritarian city state of Sparta, Athens's great rival, were considerably better off than their counterparts in the fledgeling democracy. Yet it is ironic that the women who inhabited a city famous for its innovative political system should have spent the greater part of their lives shut up in the *gynaeceum*, the women's part of the house. The reason for their seclusion is simple: women in Athens were valued even less than in comparable societies of the period because, among upper-class men, homosexual relationships were held to be far superior to those between men and women, and the female function was solely reproductive. Eva Cantarella observes:

> For the Greek man the homosexual relationship was a privileged outlet for exchange of experience, and he found in it an answer to his greatest needs. To relegate women to a purely biological role was perfectly natural.[2]

A clear account of these twin attitudes—a belief in the superiority of male homosexual relations and a corresponding lack of regard for women—is given by Walter Hamilton, former Master of Magdalene College, Cambridge, in the introduction to his translation of the *Symposium*, one of Plato's dramatic dialogues. The *Symposium* is Plato's account of a fictional dinner party, set in 416 BC, and attended by historical figures from the literati of Athens, including Socrates, the playwright Aristophanes, and Alcibiades, the Athenian general who was a protégé of Pericles. The eight men round the table pass the evening in a discussion in which it quickly becomes clear that the idea of a deep and lasting relationship between a man and a woman would have struck them as ludicrous. Hamilton writes:

> The love with which the dialogue is concerned, and which is accepted as a matter of course by all the speakers, including Socrates, is homosexual love; it is assumed without argument that this alone is capable of satisfying a man's highest and noblest aspirations, and the love of

a man and woman, when it is mentioned at all, is spoken
of as altogether inferior, a purely physical impulse whose
sole object is the procreation of children.[3]

These people did not believe, as many of us do today, that
homosexuality and heterosexuality are equally valid ways of
expressing love. Plato himself, according to Walter Hamilton,
held the view that 'a homosexual relationship is alone capable of
being transformed into a lifelong partnership'.[4] Hamilton goes on
to say that the philosopher 'presumably believed that, as things
are, women are incapable of creative activity above the physical
level'.[5]

In the dialogue, this notion is placed in the mouth of one of
the early speakers, one Pausanias, who is the lover of the host,
the poet Agathon. Pausanias avers that there are two sorts of love
and the first, the baser type, is characterized by the fact that 'it
is directed towards women quite as much as young men'.[6] Those
who are influenced by the second, higher sort of love, 'are at-
tracted towards the male sex, and value it as being naturally the
stronger and more intelligent'.[7]

When it is the turn to speak of the comic dramatist Aristophanes, he gives an account of the origin of love which does at least
accept that heterosexual and homosexual love are equally natural.
Even so, the speech given to him by Plato makes it clear that he
regards homosexual love as superior. These ideas are expressed in
a long passage in which Aristophanes explains that there were
originally three sexes on earth rather than two: male, female, and
hermaphrodite. These beings were foolish enough to attack the
gods and were punished by being split down the middle; thus all
human beings are incomplete, perpetually seeking their lost half
in a search to which we give the names of love. This, he says,
is how heterosexuality comes about:

Those men who are halves of a being of the common sex, which was called, as I told you, hermaphrodite, are lovers of women, and most adulterers come from this class, as also do women who are mad about men and sexually promiscuous.[8]

It is clear from this passage that Aristophanes regards heterosexual passion as a base emotion, a point which he emphasizes when he talks about the origins of the homosexual impulse in men (lesbians, being women, do not possess comparable virtues; they are dismissed in two brief sentences):

But those who are halves of a male whole pursue males, and being slices, so to speak, of the male, love men throughout their boyhood, and take pleasure in physical contact with men. Some people say that they are shameless, but they are wrong. It is not shamelessness which inspires their behaviour, but high spirit and manliness and virility, which lead them to welcome the society of their own kind. A striking proof of this is that such boys alone, when they reach maturity, engage in public life. When they grow to be men, they become lovers of boys, and it requires the compulsion of convention to overcome their natural disinclination to marriage and procreation; they are quite content to live with one another unwed.[9]

The link between male passion for boys and contempt for women has a striking parallel with this passage from a book published well over 2,000 years after the *Symposium*:

Homosexuality was a very prominent thing in my day. Just to show how prominent it was, when I was about

fifteen I came back from holiday, and we grouped in a
room together, about five or six of us, and I said, 'Well,
I don't know, I think women are really quite interesting,
and I'm not so sure about little boys . . . perhaps one
should forget about all this.' And everyone in the room
turned on me and said (I will never forget it), 'You
bloody pervert!' They were saying it in a half-mocking
tone, but by God I think they meant it.[10]

The speaker is the film critic Derek Malcolm, interviewed
about his schooldays in an establishment for contemporary upper-
class males, Eton College. The difference is, of course, that homosexuality at British public schools is regarded as a phase of
adolescent development, something to be got out of the way, as
Malcolm says:

If you were to ask me if any of them were gay now, I
should say they've probably naturally grown out of it
like everybody else, but I would think S— hasn't.[11]

It may be, of course, that far from 'growing out of it', the
homosexual phase at public school genuinely represents the sexuality of some of the boys—and their switch to heterosexuality
occurs because of the 'compulsion of convention', which Plato
mentioned. The effect on their attitudes to women of this enforced heterosexuality is not hard to guess; frustration and anger
eventually transform the female into the enemy. Conversely,
many openly gay men enjoy and even seek out the company of
women, and the relationship between these men and their female
friends is often refreshingly free from the distortions imposed by
'normal' masculine and feminine behaviour. This is not universally the case, however; it is a disturbing fact that many gay men

who have not succumbed to the demands of society in terms of
marriage and procreation unashamedly admit their disgust for
women. In Alan Hollinghurst's novel *The Swimming-Pool Library*, an elderly gay peer called Lord Nantwich delights in
denigrating women:

> There are chaps who don't care for [women], you know.
> Simply can't abide them. Can't stand the sight of them,
> their titties and their big sit-upons, even the smell of
> them.[12]

The novel is a voyage of discovery in which the narrator,
Will (to whom the above speech is addressed), a young, glamorous, gay man, finds out about the submerged history of homosexual men and his family's role in oppressing them. Even though
he appears to be discomfited by Nantwich's gibes against the
female sex, Will's own distaste for women emerges towards the
end of the book, if in a slightly disguised form, when he remarks
to a friend:

> And men are often like that together—I don't mean gay
> men particularly, but the sense I have that men don't
> really want women around much. I think most men are
> happiest in a male world, with gangs and best friends and
> all that.[13]

One of the most striking things about Hollinghurst's book
is the almost complete absence of women, and the sense that his
male characters inhabit a world from which women have been
deliberately excluded. Will's milieu is one of clubs (gentlemen's
or athletic), lavatories, and gay pubs in which men of all ages,
classes and races mingle on an equal basis: an admirably egalitarian

model except for its refusal to countenance the presence of the female sex. They cannot avoid women altogether, of course, unlike the gay Englishman encountered by Christopher Isherwood in Tenerife in the 1930s and mentioned by him in a letter:

> This place is a sort of monastery, anyhow. It is run by a German of the Göring-Roman Emperor type and an Englishman who dyes his hair. The Englishman loathes women so much that he has put a barbed wire entanglement across an opening in the garden wall, to keep them out.[14]

It is, perhaps, a sign of progress that by the 1930s a serious woman-hater had to shut himself up to avoid women rather than, like the Athenians, simply confining them to the house. But the homosexual coterie that dominated English literature in the 1930s certainly shared the Platonic attitude to women generally, as Isherwood's contemporary, W. H. Auden, made clear in the last stanza of a poem, entitled 'Ode to the New Year' (1939), which he sent as a gift to his friend Tom Driberg:

> Now before the party is over,
> I must mention the haters of Man,
> The passport officials at Dover,
> The military chiefs in Japan;
> To those who sold us at München.
> To those who betrayed us in Spain,
> And to all the Dictators wir wünschen
> The paralysis of the Insane;
> To Fascists, Policemen, & Women,
> Long nights on the glaciers of fear,

And a lake of brimstone to swim in;
And a BLOODY NASTY NEW YEAR.[15]

The sentiments of the poem demonstrate a remarkable piece of projection, with Auden's own dislike of women transformed into their alleged hatred of 'Man' (that the word refers specifically to the male sex could not in this case be clearer). It is also striking that Auden included 'Women' in a list of enemies made up largely of fascists; it is hard to know whether he was implying that women are the natural allies of the right, or that their effect on 'Man' is as stultifying as that political philosophy. Ironically, Auden's distaste for women is echoed in the work of an author who was a product of precisely the type of militaristic Japanese fascism to which he refers disparagingly in the poem. Yukio Mishima was a fanatically right-wing novelist and playwright who committed suicide in 1970, using the ritual form of disembowelment known as hara-kiri. The only things Mishima had in common with Auden were his homosexuality and his dislike of women, though neither were deterred from marriage. His novel *Forbidden Colours*, published in Japan in 1950, is the story of an elderly novelist, the ugly Shunsuké, who sets out to avenge the wrongs he believes he has suffered at the hands of women in his three failed marriages and ten unhappy affairs. The instrument of his revenge is a beautiful homosexual boy, Yuichi, whom Shunsuké instructs in the art of ensnaring women with the object of abandoning them. The book is packed with reflections which, though placed in the mouth of the supposedly heterosexual Shunsuké, sound like the authentic voice of the author:

Yuichi had all the gifts of youth the old writer lacked, but at the same time he had that supreme good fortune the artist had always hypothesized as the object of his heart's desire. In short, he had never loved a woman . . . If Shunsuké had been like Yuichi in his youth, what joy there would have been in his love of women. And if like Yuichi he had not loved a woman—suppose, better yet, he had come to live without women—what a happy life his would have been![16]

For some gay men, their dislike of women extends beyond the female sex to anything associated with femaleness or femininity. Just such an aversion is forcefully expressed in Compton Mackenzie's novel *Thin Ice*, published in 1956 when sex between men was still illegal in Britain. Henry, a parliamentary candidate, is talking to a friend about the way in which he is able to conceal his sexuality:

> Thank God, I am completely masculine, and shall be able to pass for one of those Victorian woman-haters. The poor devils who are half women have a much harder task than mine. And I am such a woman-hater that they are as displeasing to me as woman herself.[17]

Fear of the female, a physical aversion to women, has been a constant feature of homosexual literature from Plato to the present day. In Alan Hollinghurst's outspoken novel, *The Swimming-Pool Library*, the celebration of the male body in defiance of the onset of AIDS and a more reactionary moral climate, in itself an admirable statement of gay rights, is done so repetitiously and pointedly that, by the end of the book, it has begun to feel uncomfortably like denial, a manifesto for a woman-free future—one that would be, for the female sex, nothing less than a retreat into the *gynaeceum* and the past.

1 Eva Cantarella, *Pandora's Daughters: The Role and Status of Women in Greek and Roman Antiquity*, Johns Hopkins, 1987, p. 46.

2 Ibid., pp. 85–6.

3 Plato, *The Symposium*, translated by Walter Hamilton, Penguin, 1951, p. 12.

4 Ibid., p. 13.

5 Ibid., p. 23.

6 Ibid., p. 46.

7 Ibid., p. 47.

8 Ibid., p. 62.

9 Ibid., pp. 62–3.

10 Danny Danziger, *Eton Voices*, Viking, 1988, p. 199.

11 Ibid., p. 206.

12 Alan Hollinghurst, *The Swimming-Pool Library*, Chatto and Windus, 1988, p. 37 (Random House, 1989).

13 Ibid., p. 242.

14 Quoted in John Lehmann, *Christopher Isherwood: A Personal Memoir*, Weidenfeld and Nicolson, 1987.

15 W. H. Auden, *'Ode to the New Year'*, 1939, Weidenfeld and Nicolson, 1987 (Auden file, Driberg Archive, Christ Church College, Oxford). Auden's literary executor, Edward Mendelson, gave permission to quote from this poem on condition that I include this note: 'The antipathy to women expressed in this stanza suddenly appeared in Auden's unpublished writings in August 1938, and lasted for a period of about five months. During the same period he expressed a comparably intense antipathy to the English people. Both antipathies (effectively rejections of his family) arose from an intense discontent over his emotional life, and both disappeared when he moved to America and fell in love with Chester Kallman early in 1939. In 1941, in Part II of "The Temptation of St Joseph" in *For the Time Being*, Auden explicitly renounced the misogyny he had expressed in 1938.'

16 Yukio Mishima, *Forbidden Colours*, Penguin, 1971, p. 34 (Putnam, 1981).

17 Compton Mackenzie, *Thin Ice*, Chatto and Windus, 1956, p. 55.

# CZECH MATE

Charlotte Brontë's novel *Shirley,* published in 1849, contains a passionate denunciation of the author of *Paradise Lost.* 'Milton was great', Shirley Keeldar concedes, 'but was he good?' Her charge against the blind poet is quite specific—that his prolific imagination was able to summon up heaven, hell, Satan, Sin, Death, whole armies of angels and devils, but not Eve. 'Milton tried to see the first woman', Shirley tells her friend and confidante Caroline Helstone, 'but, Cary, he saw her not'. Instead:

> It was his cook that he saw; or it was Mrs Gill, as I have seen her, making custards, in the heat of summer, in the cool dairy, with rose-trees and nasturtiums about the latticed window, preparing a cold collation for the rectors,—preserves, and 'dulcet creams' . . .[1]

The obvious answer to Shirley's charge, that Milton was unable to envisage a model of womanhood other than the domestic, is that he was reflecting real life—that the vast majority of seventeenth-century English women were expected to, and did, confine themselves to the home. Yet there was, if Milton had wanted it, another and quite different example at hand in the shape of Elizabeth I, whose death in 1603 preceded Milton's birth by only five years. That monarch, though childless, approximates much more closely to the glorious 'woman-Titan' of Shirley's imagination than Milton's compliant housewife, which suggests that the poet's failure of vision in *Paradise Lost* was not quite so inevitable as it might at first seem.

The Czech novelist Milan Kundera was born in 1929, more than three centuries after Milton. He, too, is regarded as 'great', insofar as such judgments are made of living writers; his novels appear garlanded with tributes from novelists like Ian McEwan and Salman Rushdie. McEwan described *The Unbearable Lightness of Being* as 'a dark and brilliant achievement', while Rushdie saluted *The Book of Laughter and Forgetting* as 'a masterpiece'; he was even more fulsome in his praise of *The Joke,* hailing its author as 'clearly one of the best to be found anywhere . . . It is impossible to do justice here to the subtleties, comedy and wisdom of this very beautiful novel'.

The front cover of the King Penguin edition of *The Joke* shows a man in shirtsleeves; unusually, there are no naked women in sight. The same publisher chose a female torso, naked except for a black suspender belt, for *The Book of Laughter and Forgetting,* and another female nude, breasts concealed by her arms, for *The Farewell Party.* In one instance the greater part of the face is concealed in shadow, in the other it is completely cut off by a black bar; this theme of female muteness is taken one step further by Faber's hardback edition of *Immortality,* which depicts the headless upper torso of a woman with curious brown streamers emerging from her severed neck. These are clever images: grainy, slightly perplexing (why has the woman on the cover of *The Book of Laughter and Forgetting* been given wings in place of her left arm?), and therefore conveying the message that the subject matter of the books is the intellectually acceptable one of sexuality rather than common-or-garden sex. Reviewers have responded to these visual prompts, discerning in Kundera's writing 'a hedonist's love of eroticism, fantasy and fun'—Salman Rushdie on *The Book of Laughter and Forgetting*— yet in doing so they have overlooked the obvious and contradictory fact of his distaste for the female. Here are some images of women, chosen more or less at random from Kundera's novels:

> She was sitting there on the toilet, and her sudden desire to void her bowels was in fact a desire to go to the extreme of humiliation, to become only and utterly a body, the body her mother used to say was good for nothing but digesting and excreting. And as she voided her bowels, Tereza was overcome by a feeling of infinite grief and loneliness. Nothing could be more miserable than her naked body perched on the enlarged end of a sewer pipe. *(The Unbearable Lightness of Being* [2] *)*

> . . . she felt an instinctive distaste for the female multitude which reduced the worth of an individual woman as such. She was surrounded by a depressing glut of breasts, an inflation that made even a bosom as shapely as hers lose value. *(The Farewell Party* [3] *)*

> They yearned to torpedo the glory of feminine beauty, for they knew that in the last analysis one body is more or less like another, and ugliness revenges itself against beauty by whispering in a man's ear: Look, this is the real truth of that feminine figure you find so bewitching! Look, this repellent, sagging mammary gland is the same thing as that shapely breast you so foolishly adore! *(The Farewell Party* [4] *)*

Breasts, breasts and more breasts; here is a man who cannot see a woman for her mammary glands. (No wonder Kundera's publishers flaunt them on his covers.) The final passage quoted above is particularly revealing, for it suggests one of the reasons for Kundera's dislike of women: *their bodies let you down*. The most attractive woman ages, and how disgusting older women are:

> Women were sitting around the edge of the basin like huge frogs. Olga was afraid of them. All of them were older than she, they were bigger, had more fat and skin. She sat down humbly among them, hunched into herself and frowning. *(The Farewell Party* [5]*)*

> In a moment [Agnes] lost sight of the couple and instead saw in front of her a woman dressed in baggy trousers barely reaching the knees, as was the fashion that year. The outfit seemed to make her behind even heavier and closer to the ground. Her bare, pale calves resembled a pair of rustic pitchers decorated by varicose veins entwined like a ball of tiny blue snakes. *(Immortality* [6]*)*

The attentive reader will have noticed that the protagonist in both these passages is female, a device whose purpose is to universalise Kundera's disgust and suggest it is shared by the objects of it. The same device is used even more explicitly, and transparently, in the next passage, in which a female character reflects on the (allegedly) graceless way in which women age; a woman, she muses, is like 'a poor machinanic ordered to keep a small factory running':

> . . . the more useless a woman's body becomes, the more it is a body: heavy and burdensome; it resembles an old factory destined for demolition, which the woman's self must watch to the very end, like a caretaker. *(Immortality* [7]*)*

Characterisation has never been Kundera's strong point, but how many woman go through life comparing themselves to a disused factory? The cumulative effect of these passages, in which character after character offers some variation on the same theme of the inadequacy of the female body, is to raise the question of why Kundera is so obsessed with it. The need to belittle and to denigrate, not once but repeatedly, suggests a response activated by more than the aesthetic; Kundera's characters protest too much, make such a show of their contempt, that it is hard not to believe they are hiding something. What that might be is suggested both by common sense and by a vivid scene in which we see a man 'making love' to a woman from behind:

> He had the feeling that the leap he had just taken was a leap across endless time, the leap of a little boy hurtling his way from childhood to manhood. And as he moved on her, each time he went back and forth, he felt he was describing the movement from childhood to maturity and back, the movement from a boy staring powerless at an enormous female body to a man gripping that body and taming it. (The Book of Laughter and Forgetting [8])

The issue, as one might expect, is power; each time a character in a Kundera novel pours scorn on the female body, he or she—and we have seen that the author sometimes adopts a female disguise—is denying the fear that that body inspires. 'Afraid of those sagging breasts, those varicosed calves, that flabby belly? Not me!' Yet the adult man who responds to women in this way, who construes his life as a struggle against what he sees as their excessive power, can never be *quite* certain that he has tamed the terrifying female body. He has constantly to think up ways of proving his mastery, such as this:

I turned her head to one side; then to the other; I turned
it back and forth several times, and suddenly the motion
became a slap; and a second; and a third. Helena began
to sob and moan, but with excitement, not pain; her chin
strained up to find me, and I beat her and beat her and
beat her; then I saw her breasts straining upward as well
and (arching up over her) beat her all over her arms and
sides and breast. . . . *(The Joke* 9*)*

Public humiliation will do just as well, as in this scene in
which a woman collecting for charity in a Paris Metro station
is forced to dance with two drunks:

She wanted to defend herself but she could not take her
eyes off the portly man who was smiling encouragement;
when she tried to return his smile, the *clochard* lifted her
skirt waist high: this revealed her bare legs and green
panties (an excellent match for the pink skirt). *(Immortality* 10*)*

Voyeurism of this sort has two satisfactory outcomes: it
exposes the despised object, woman, to ridicule *and* justifies the
contempt of the spectator by emphasising her enjoyment of it.
Agnes, the female character who was so dismayed by her own
body in one of the passages quoted above, is later the subject of
an erotic fantasy in which she is crucified naked before a huge,
baying crowd:

She saw her own image, the image of a woman on a cross
with extended arms and bare breasts, she was exposed to
the immense, shouting, bestial crowd, and along with the
crowd she gazed, excited, at herself. *(Immortality* 11*)*

This is woman's Calvary, at which her inescapable carnality, rather than her mortality, is exposed—and she loves it. Where Milton's failure of vision confined women to the role of servant, Kundera is blind to women's humanity—which they share with men—because he cannot see beyond their sexuality. His female characters are stereotypes: greedy bitches determined to get what they can out of men (Ruzena in *The Farewell Party;* Bettina Brentano in *Immortality*), rivals for the same man (Tereza and Sabina in *The Unbearable Lightness of Being;* Laura wanting, and getting, her sister's husband in *Immortality*). What they are never allowed to be is friends, with each other or with men; women in Kundera's novels exist only in relation to men, and that relation constantly reveals itself as antagonistic. That this is so, even in an apparently 'innocent, asexual' friendship, is illustrated by a scene from one of the novels in which the narrator, about to go into political exile, transfers his impotent rage against the Communist state onto a woman friend who has taken considerable risks to help him survive the regime:

> And now suddenly the butcher knife of fear had slit her open. She was as open to me as the carcass of a heifer slit down the middle and hanging on a hook. There we were, sitting side by side on a couch in a borrowed apartment, the gurgling of the water filling the empty toilet tank in the background, and suddenly I felt a violent desire to make love to her. Or to be more exact, a violent desire to rape her. *(The Book of Laughter and Forgetting* [12]*)*

This is not to argue that Kundera or his narrator are potential rapists; what it does expose is an underlying hostility to women which allows them to substitute with alarming ease for the real, untouchable enemy. Hostility is the common factor in all Kundera's writing about women, and the only difference between his fiction and his nonfiction is that in the latter it operates not by denigration but by exclusion.

*The Art of the Novel,* published in French in 1986 and in English two years later, is described by its British publisher, Faber, as Kundera's 'personal conception of the European novel.' An admiring notice in the *London Review of Books* claimed that 'Kundera's map of the development of the European novel is outlined with the reckless brevity of the man who knows exactly what and where the salient points are'. The 'salient points' are those authors Kundera considers important: Richardson, Flaubert, Cervantes, Balzac, Joyce, Broch, Thomas Mann, Kafka, Proust, Sterne, Diderot, Gogol, Bely, Novalis, Musil, Aragon, Fuentes, Goethe, Laclos, Constant, Stendhal, Tolstoy, Skvorecky, Fielding. Only one female author gets a mention in *The Art of the Novel,* and that consists of a patronising aside about Agatha Christie ('The opposite of serious art is light art, minor art. But for my part, I never minded Agatha Christie's detective novels'.[13]).

Not only are novelists like Jane Austen and Charlotte Brontë ignored, Kundera writes as if they had never existed. His claim that 'with Flaubert, [the novel] explores the *terra* previously *incognita* of the everyday' is patently absurd; in *Shirley,* published eight years before *Madame Bovary,* Charlotte Brontë created a character, Caroline Helstone, who is driven into anorexic decline precisely by the tedium of everyday life. His assertion that 'the potential of Flaubert's discovery of the quotidian was only fully developed seventy years later, in James Joyce's gigantic work', compounds the error, wilfully overlooking novels like George Eliot's *Middlemarch.* This is biological determinism of the most extreme sort, one which claims for men alone the life of the mind and dismisses all evidence of female creativity. Charlotte Brontë's heroine, Shirley, thought that Milton's 'brain was right' but demanded 'how was his heart?' I do not think it requires a great leap of the imagination to work out what she would have made of Kundera's.

1. The 'dulcet creams' appear in Book V of *Paradise Lost,* in which Eve is instructed by Adam to prepare a feast for God's emissary, the angel Raphaël.
2. *The Unbearable Lightness of Being,* Penguin, 1984, pp. 156–57
3. *The Farewell Party,* Penguin, 1984, p. 27
4. Ibid, p. 101
5. Ibid, p. 99
6. *Immortality,* Faber, 1991, p. 22
7. Ibid, p. 109
8. *The Book of Laughter and Forgetting,* Penguin, 1983, p. 218
9. *The Joke,* Penguin, 1984, p. 172
10. Op cit, p. 174
11. Ibid, p. 363
12. Op cit, p. 75
13. *The Art of the Novel,* Faber, 1988, p. 135

# GENTLEMEN PREFER
# DEAD BLONDES

Here comes Marilyn, the misogynist's monster mate: those wiggling hips, that imprisoned waist, the jutting, inescapable breasts. What is she other than a woman made for sex? Yet not even a woman; the simple, naïve mind of a child has been transplanted into the body of a full-grown woman. Sex with her would be like eating ice-cream, Norman Mailer wrote.[1] He was wrong; more like taking sweets from a child in the park. Marilyn is the victim who will not, cannot, answer back, and sex with her is a paedophiliac dream: do what you like and she won't tell. How could she run to Mummy when she knows, deep inside, that she led you on, she *made* you do it?

Oh yes she did, and it's a paradox that killed her. The lonely, ignored child who never knew a stable home grew into a woman with a lust, a burning desire—but for power, not for sex. She pursued it in the only way she knew, single-mindedly exploiting her sole asset like a foolhardy miner who dares to work a deeper seam than his safety-minded colleagues, never divining that the success she sought contained within it her inevitable destruction. For the power that Norma Jeane Mortensen coveted was only the power to be a victim; the sexual exhibitionism which seemed to enslave men in reality made victims not of them but of herself.

And to what lengths was she willing to go, in pursuit of that momentary high when she could bask in the adulation of her fans and admirers, blanking out the knowledge of what they really

wanted to do to—not with, never with—the animated doll
called Marilyn Monroe. Many an aspiring starlet changed the
colour of her hair or fixed her teeth; Norma Jeane ruthlessly
re-created herself as the West's most enduring sex symbol. Look
at her in 1945, in a photograph by André de Dienes:[2] a gauche
nineteen-year-old whose idea of sexiness is to knot her blouse
below her unremarkable breasts and thrust her hips provocatively
to one side, her knicker elastic defiantly visible above the waist-
band of her stiff new jeans. Her springy brown hair is artlessly
scraped back from her face, and the shiny red lipstick she has
applied accentuates her strong white teeth. The metamorphosis
into Marilyn Monroe, movie star, seems a leap far beyond this
pert but unknowing girl, yet she managed it. She bleached her
hair, and straightened it; she had work done on those large teeth;
she underwent plastic surgery to shorten her nose and firm up her
chin; she wore her clothes a size too small; she even doctored her
shoes, cutting a bit off one heel so she would walk with a
perpetual wiggle. Told that her smile wasn't right (it's the most
natural thing about her in that 1945 picture), she made a conscious effort to do it a different way.

Her dedication to maintaining the right image knew no
bounds. The film of *Some Like It Hot*, which she made in 1958
with Tony Curtis and Jack Lemmon, was set, nominally, in 1929.
This was simply a crude device to make the most of Marilyn's
curvy, feminine figure; while the other female characters—and
her male co-stars, who are required by the plot to spend much
of their time disguised as women—appear in straight-up-and-
down flapper dresses, Marilyn's costumes are completely out of
period and skin-tight, so much so that she could not sit down in
between takes on the set. The dresses were not only ludicrous but
lethal: a matter of weeks after filming ended, she lost the baby
she had been expecting with her third husband, Arthur Miller.

Perhaps she thought it was worth it; her portrayal of the baby-voiced and feather-brained Sugar Kane, in its own way as much a travesty of womanhood as the intentionally comic drag performances of Curtis and Lemmon, is often cited as her acting triumph. But it is hardly surprising that a woman who drove herself so mercilessly was frequently brutal to other people: her career was punctuated by her dismissals both of people who worked for her and, in another sense, of friends, lovers and husbands who had outlived their usefulness.

And yet there is a haunting sadness about her photographs. They have a plaintive quality, eloquent of incoherent longing and unfulfilled hope. In picture after picture, a wistful Marilyn stares at the camera in a mute appeal for affection—just a little of it, the look says, I wouldn't take up *much* of your time. These silent appeals, effective as they are, constitute a lie. Marilyn Monroe's tragedy, in so far as there is one, is that she got everything she wanted—and then it turned out to be not what she wanted after all. Power over men, yes; but not the vicious, dribbling lust that lay behind the awed glances, the respectful introductions, the admiring eyes. Sometimes not even behind: in his autobiography, *Timebends*,[3] Arthur Miller describes how, in a bookshop, he once saw a man watching Marilyn from the next aisle while masturbating in his trousers. No wonder she was reluctant to meet Norman Mailer, the man who most perfectly understood the desires and fantasies she aroused; and no wonder that the highlight of her life, as she later described it, was her morale-boosting trip to Korea in 1954.

The episode[4] took place during what was supposed to be a wedding trip to Japan with her second husband, Joe DiMaggio. Marilyn left him behind and flew to Seoul in bitterly cold weather. From there she travelled by helicopter to visit the encampments of a US marine and a US army division. As the helicopter approached the landing-strip, Marilyn lay down on the floor and lowered her body out of a sliding door to wave to the men gathered below. Predictably, there was a near-riot as the air force police struggled to hold back the tide of men shouting her name.

Once she was safely on the ground, Marilyn paused to change into a low-cut, sequinned dress which could not have been less suited to the weather. Then she launched into a concert, regaling the troops with her version of the Gershwin song 'Do It Again', which provoked a second outburst of frenzy, so much so that an officer intervened and asked her to tone down her material. Marilyn was indignant, protesting that she'd performed 'Do It Again' 'as a straight, wistful love song'.

The claim is manifestly disingenuous; no woman squeezes herself into a tight dress, appears on stage before thousands of soldiers who have been isolated from female company for months, and presents them with a suggestive song without knowing exactly what she's doing. But Marilyn wasn't practising a straightforward deception. The illusion that the audience was excited only by its admiration for her was her life-blood, as necessary to her as the admiration itself: she was the visiting goddess, the untouchable idol who had graciously given up time on her wedding trip—yes, even on her wedding trip—to gratify her respectful fans. If things had got out of hand, it certainly wasn't *her* fault. 'I'd been up against this sort of thing before,' she later wrote in her autobiography.[5] 'People had a habit of looking at me as if I were some kind of mirror instead of a person. They didn't see me, they saw their own lewd thoughts. Then they white-masked themselves by calling me the lewd one.'

It's a half-perceptive statement; Monroe acted as a focal point for male fantasies about women. (Her powerful and undoubted appeal for women is, of course, a different matter: she inspires an uneasy blend of awe, envy and sympathy.) She had done her best to erase her own distinguishing features: she bleached her hair, and kept out of the sun in order to keep her skin as pale as possible; she dressed in white whenever she could. All that was left was the shape of a woman, exaggerated and emphasized by the constricting clothes—sometimes reminiscent of the bondage outfits associated with sado-masochistic ritual—she wore. She was not so much woman-as-mirror as woman-as-blank. She offered men an outline, a blank form on which they could scribble their fantasies about what a woman should be like. Then, when they'd made her into the creature of their desires, she invited them to act out those fantasies—'Do It Again'—without demanding anything in return.

It was precisely this aspect of her image—her promise of no demands, no demurrals—that fascinated Norman Mailer. By the time he embarked on his massive and revealing biography of the star she was long dead, safe from the stark message of his repellent, panting prose. 'She would ask no price,'[6] he slavered:

> She was not the dark contract of those passionate brunette depths that speak of blood, vows taken for life, and the furies of vengeance if you are untrue to the depth of passion, no, Marilyn suggested sex might be difficult and dangerous with others, but ice-cream with her.

There it is, that curiously haunting and vivid image: Marilyn as ice-cream, a child's afternoon treat, cheap and quickly consumed (not to mention cold—an unconscious association of her unresponsiveness, her fantasized lack of demands, with frigidity?). Mailer looks at Monroe and, he writes, sees a woman who is saying: 'Take me. I'm easy. I'm happy. I'm an angel of sex, you bet.'[7] He watches her provocative walk, her hips swinging from side to side, and gets the message: 'Take me from behind, I'm yours.'[8] He gazes at a publicity still and hears her whisper: 'You can fuck me if you like, Mr Sugar.'[9]

The source of Marilyn's appeal, for Mailer, is her absolute passivity. She is as defenceless as a child, a woman to whom a man can do *anything* in the name of sex, secure in the knowledge that she will never complain. She certainly won't demand any degree of reciprocity ('I'm happy'). The contradiction of her achievement, for Marilyn, is now all too plain: her hard work, her sacrifices, the discarded husbands and lovers, the abortions and miscarried pregnancies, have arrived at this, that she is valued only for her lack of value. Her power is weakest when her success is complete. *Of course* that realization is unbearable; *of course* she is unhappy.

And what of the men, the fans who drool over her image, what do they get from this sterile exchange? Something of extraordinary potency, if we are to judge by Marilyn Monroe's enduring appeal. Her image, the pointy breasts and the wiggling rear, take on a tinge of horror for women who understand the meaning of her spectacular success. By turning herself into an icon of female passivity, she had studio bosses, directors, sportsmen, intellectuals, politicians and princes at her feet. Her popularity represents a rejection of mutuality in sex in favour of a pattern of male dominance and female submission. For that reason alone, it is difficult to sympathize with her; certainly those biographies which depict her as a sweet, misunderstood human being, a gifted actress destroyed by the inflexibility of the studio bosses, are pretty wide of the mark. Monroe was tough, and her behaviour was often little better than that of the spoilt child, the darling daughter, that she aped in the public presentation of her sexuality. But she was a victim, and in a double sense: as the object of male sexual fantasies of a peculiarly horrible kind, and in her failure

to see the poisoned nature of the chalice for which she was
striving.

Turning herself into Marilyn Monroe gave Norma Jeane
Mortensen fame, adulation, money—and an extremely limited
shelf life. Monroe is unlike other women not only in her unusual
blankness, her lack of definition, but in her inability to grow old.
Unlike the working-class women among whom she grew up,
unlike even the real actresses she met through her work, Monroe
was too fragile a product to mature with age. The process of
ageing would, in itself, mean failure: the paedophiliac loses interest as his victim grows up.

By the time Marilyn understood the corner into which she
had driven herself, it was too late. Accustomed to deriving what
power she had from men—the millions who made up her fans—
she could formulate solutions to her difficulty only in the same
narrow terms. Since she could not hope forever to hold her appeal
for the mass of men, she sought to use her looks, while she still
had them, to secure the permanent attention of just one. But not
any old one: it is symptomatic of her adulation of glamour that,
fearing the eventual fading of her own, she sought to attach it
to herself at one remove. The first man she married after her rise
to star status was Joe DiMaggio, America's top baseball player;
significantly, DiMaggio was a celebrity who had succeeded in
retiring and yet remaining an admired and attention-drawing
public figure. When that marriage failed to work, she turned to
a man who was famous in another field, the playwright Arthur
Miller. Finally, at the end of her life, she seems to have enter-
tained illusory hopes of marrying the President's younger
brother, the US Attorney General Bobby Kennedy. The most
likely explanation of her death is that, following Kennedy's break
with her, she staged yet another suicide attempt. This time, no
one came to the rescue.

In a perverse way, Marilyn's death was the logical next step in her career as a sex symbol. By dying when her looks had only just begun to fade, she removed at a stroke the possibility of other, older images replacing those she had assiduously peddled to the public during her years as a movie star; if she were alive now she would be—unthinkable thought—the same age as the Queen. She left behind a mystery, a tantalizing sequence of events on the night of her death, which is as good a story as Hollywood ever offered her. But, above and beyond everything else, she guaranteed forever the passivity of her sexual response by imbuing it with the glamorous stillness of death. After all, isn't paedophilia next to necrophilia?

1 Norman Mailer, *Marilyn: A Biography*, Putnam Publishing Group, 1987, p. 15.
2 Ibid., p. 40.
3 Arthur Miller, *Timebends: A Life*, Methuen, 1987, p. 306 (Grove, 1987).
4 These events are described in detail in Fred Lawrence Guiles, *Norma Jeane: The Life and Death of Marilyn Monroe*, Grafton, 1986, pp. 251–2.
5 Marilyn Monroe, *My Story*, Stein and Day, 1986, pp. 237–8.
6 Norman Mailer, op. cit., p. 15.
7 Ibid., p. 15.
8 Ibid., p. 79.
9 Ibid., p. 91.

# HOLOCAUST
# GIRLS

William Styron is a white author from the American South. He has impeccable liberal credentials: in 1968 he was among nearly 500 intellectuals who risked a fine or imprisonment by pledging to withhold that portion of their income tax which would be spent in furtherance of the Vietnam war.

His fame as an author stems primarily from his long novel *Sophie's Choice*, the story of a young Polish woman who survived incarceration in Auschwitz. But an earlier Styron book, *The Confessions of Nat Turner* (1967), provoked an outcry among black Americans. The novel is the fictional 'autobiography' of a historical figure, the black leader of a slave revolt in Virginia. A book of essays, *William Styron's Nat Turner: Ten Black Writers Respond*, laid a variety of charges against Styron, including racism and falsification of history. The most interesting complaint was that Styron had chosen to insert into the story a completely fictional black character who is eager to rape women. As the historian and novelist David Caute remarked in a discussion of the controversy over the Nat Turner book, 'no rape did occur during the real Nat Turner's slave revolt, so why inject this element?'[1]

The tale is instructive, both as evidence of Styron's approach to historical material and as an example of the form that his embellishments might take. For *Sophie's Choice*, Styron's later book about the Holocaust (it was first published in Britain in

1979), is also presented as a fictionalized account of real events, this time Styron's own involvement immediately after the Second World War with a concentration-camp survivor. It received rave reviews on both sides of the Atlantic: the *Washington Star* described it as 'breathtaking'; the *New Statesman* hailed it as 'a novel of stunning audacity and imaginative range'. The paperback version was reprinted several times, and the film director Alan J. Pakula turned it into a movie, with Meryl Streep playing Sophie.

The book is, nevertheless, not what it seems. And all those people who were impressed by its 'immediacy', 'scale' and 'mesmeric strength' fell for it. It isn't hard to see why. Styron is a skilful narrator, and he makes liberal use of the stock device of constantly hinting that further revelations are to come ('But now it again becomes necessary to mention that Sophie was not quite straightforward in her recital of past events . . . I would learn this later . . .'[2]). More crucial to the book's success, however, is its breaking of taboo: its central theme, the Holocaust, is a subject rarely addressed in fiction. Authors have, on the whole, left writing about the mass murder of Jews, gypsies, homosexuals, members of various Resistance movements, and others by the Nazis to historians and to survivors like Primo Levi. There is a sense that to 'use the terrible fact of the camps for emotional and aesthetic effect',[3] in Paul Bailey's phrase from his introduction to *If This Is A Man* and *The Truce*, is to cheapen the experience of millions who cannot speak for themselves. Any writer who, like Styron, overcomes this hesitation is bound to reap the harvest of others' reticence; simply because there are so few novels about the camps, his will stand out.

But why stop at one taboo when you can break another? The most startling thing about *Sophie's Choice* is that it is a relentlessly eroticized narrative: the female characters in it—principally the Auschwitz survivor, Sophie—exist as stimulants of lust in Stingo, the Styron-identified character; either directly, through their physical presence, or indirectly as Stingo/Styron hears about (or, indeed, overhears) their sexual exploits with other people. One of the book's major themes is Stingo's frustrated attempts to achieve full intercourse in addition to his single and unsatisfactory experience with a prostitute (apart, that is, from the encounters with 'nasty little Protestants who had so tortured me in the back seats of a score of cars'[4]). We hear in detail[5] about his attempts to penetrate Leslie Lapidus, 'a hot-skinned, eager-bellied Jewish girl with fathomless eyes and magnificent apricot-and-ocher suntanned legs that all but promised to squeeze the life out of me'.[6] When the dirty-talking Leslie proves less compliant than he had anticipated, Stingo transfers his hopes to one Mary Alice Grimball, only to find that his desire is once again to remain unfulfilled. For Mary Alice is 'something *worse* than a Cock Tease, a Whack-off artist'.[7] While she steadfastly refuses to allow Stingo access to 'any of the more interesting crannies or recesses of her incredibly desirable body',[8] she *is* willing 'to whack me off hour after hour until I am a lifeless and juiceless stalk'.[9] These sexual interludes are interspersed with details of Sophie's life in the concentration camp; indeed, at one point, death-camp imagery suddenly invades an erotic passage. As Stingo grapples fruitlessly with Leslie on a couch, he at last manages to grasp a bare breast which 'felt like a soggy ball of dough beneath my hand, itself tightly imprisoned within the rim of a murderous brassiere made of wormwood and wire'.[10] Here we have the secret of the novel's popularity: the juxtaposition of sex and the Holocaust has been dressed up as art, thus sanctioning its passage from the back room to the shelves reserved for the literary ('. . . *Sophie's Choice* has to be regarded as one of the few great novels of post-war American literature'—John F. Baker, former editor of the American trade journal *Publisher's Weekly*).

Styron has, of course, prepared his ground carefully. The novel is, remember, a 'true' story; all he is doing is recalling real events. His narrator, Stingo, gives an account in Chapter Nine of the novel's genesis, and it seems likely that it is an accurate description of how the book came into existence:

> For twenty years Sophie and Sophie's life . . . and all the interconnected and progressively worsening circumstances which led that poor straw-haired Polish darling headlong into destruction had preyed on my memory like a repetitive and ineradicable tic.[11]

By 1967, Stingo/Styron says, he was 'thinking in earnest' about Sophie's story; several more years were to pass before 'I began the story . . . as it has been set down here'.

The story, in essence, is this (although it takes Styron 684 pages to get through it): Stingo, an impoverished would-be writer from the deep South, takes a room in a boarding-house in Brooklyn just after the end of the Second World War. Among the other boarders are Sophie and her lover Nathan, a highly intelligent research biologist. The relationship between the two lovers is explosively sexual and violent; Stingo's first sight of Sophie comes during a row as Nathan heaps abuse on her.

> 'Don't give me any of *that*, you hear,' I heard him yell. 'You're a liar! You're a miserable lying cunt, do you hear me? A *cunt*!'
>
> 'You're a cunt, too,' I heard her throw back at him.

'Yes, you're a cunt, I think.' Her tone lacked aggressive-
ness.

'I am *not* a cunt,' he roared. 'I *can't* be a cunt, you
dumb fucking Polack. When are you going to learn to
*speak* the *language*? A *prick* I might be, but not a *cunt*,
you moron. Don't you ever call me that again, you hear?
Not that you'll ever get a chance.'

'You called *me* that!'

'But that's what you *are*, you moron—a two-timing,
double-crossing cunt! Spreading that twat of yours for
a cheap, chiseling quack doctor. Oh *God*!' he howled,
and his voice rose in wild uncontained rage. 'Let me out
of here before I *murder* you—you *whore*! You were *born*
a whore and you'll *die* a whore!'[12]

Undeterred by this tirade, Stingo falls 'swiftly and fathom-
lessly in love' with Sophie, although his affection for her manifests itself in a self-obsessed form which seems to have more to
do with lust than affection. As he gets to know her better, he
discovers that during her stay at Auschwitz she, a non-Jew,
pretended to be an anti-Semite in the hope of saving herself and
her little boy, and that she made a clumsy attempt to seduce the
camp commandant, Rudolf Höss, while working in his house as
his secretary.

Meanwhile, as the summer wears on, Stingo's attempts to
gain sexual experience come to nothing. The relationship between Sophie and Nathan degenerates still further, to the point
where he rejects her and disappears from the boarding-house.
Stingo now discovers that, far from being a research biologist,
Nathan is a paranoid schizophrenic and a danger to Sophie. He
hauls the devastated woman off on a journey to his home in the

South, during which the novel reaches its double climax. In a cheap Washington hotel, Sophie finally reveals the source of her anguished guilt: on arriving at Auschwitz, a Nazi doctor told her to choose which of her two children was to survive; if she refused to make the choice, both would die. Stingo's sympathetic reaction to this harrowing story (Sophie kept her little boy, only to have him disappear forever into the children's camp) is to take her out for a meal and then fuck her back at the hotel. Next morning he wakes to find her missing. She is on her way to Nathan, and both are shortly found dead in an apparent suicide pact.

There are two ways of looking at this narrative. The first, which is probably how Styron intends us to see it, is that the story is a painfully honest account of a tragic episode in which his younger self struggled, but failed, to save Sophie from the doom that was rushing towards her. That is certainly how the *Washington Star* saw it: 'It is a novel rooted in the "facts" of Styron's own life and that of a young woman he once knew, and this makes its force all the more breathtaking.' But if this is the correct interpretation, it is difficult to read the book without continually cursing Styron/Stingo for his failure to give Sophie the help she needs; confronted with her despair and anguish, the narrator's main concern remains his now urgent sexual appetite. True, the two pages of fucking and sucking which precede Sophie's final flight to Nathan are initiated by her ('The varieties of sexual experience are, I suppose, so multifarious that it is an exaggeration to say that Sophie and I did that night everything it is possible to do. But I'll swear we came close . . .';[13]) but it is Stingo's determination to drag her down South and possess her, instead of stopping to consider her blindingly obvious needs—a love that, far from being primarily sexual, is willing to give her time and space to express her grief and guilt—which puts her into a situation where her only choices are between life with a man she doesn't love and death with one she does. The novel betrays very little sense that Stingo/Styron is aware of his complicity in Sophie's death; indeed, the narrator specifically excuses himself:

> As with most unspeakable events, there were certain troublesome 'ifs' involved, making it all the more painful, in retrospect, to ponder the ways in which the whole thing might have been prevented. (Not that I think it really could have been prevented, in the end.[14])

The key to the other way of seeing *Sophie's Choice* is provided by what we know about Styron's earlier book, *The Confessions of Nat Turner*. Here, remember, one of the charges against him was that he had introduced into the narrative a completely fictitious character, and one who brought an ahistorical sexual element into the book (his urge to rape women). Here, then, is evidence of Styron's tendency to embroider for erotic purposes; could it be that what he is really doing in telling Sophie's story is using tragic events as a vehicle for sexual fantasies which would otherwise be condemned as belonging on the unacceptable side of the boundary between literature and porn? Let's examine the evidence.

Just before Stingo/Styron meets Sophie, he learns that his childhood sweetheart, a woman called Maria Hunt, has leapt to her death from a building in Manhattan. His response, after brooding on the news, is an intensely erotic dream in which 'my departed Maria was standing before me, with the abandon of a strumpet stripping down to the flesh—she who had never removed in my presence so much as her bobbysocks.'[15] The naked Maria proceeds to suck Stingo's cock until he awakes abruptly to the noise of Sophie and Nathan fucking in the room above him.

It is immediately after the Maria Hunt dream that Stingo first meets and falls in love with Sophie, in the midst of that terrible row with Nathan:

> It was a love which, as time wore on that summer, I realized had many reasons for laying claim to my existence. But I must confess that at first, certainly one of them was her distant but real resemblance to Maria Hunt. And what is still ineffaceable about my first glimpse of her is not simply the lovely simulacrum she seemed to me of the dead girl but the despair on her face worn as Maria surely must have worn it, along with the premonitory, grieving shadows of someone hurtling headlong toward death.[16]

In passage after passage Stingo/Styron harps on his knowledge that Sophie is doomed:

> Then again I fell asleep, only to wake with a start just before dawn, in the dead silence of that hour, with pounding heart and an icy chill staring straight up at my ceiling above which Sophie slept, understanding with a dreamer's fierce clarity that she was doomed.[17]

This 'knowledge' is, in fact, the source of the narrator's obsessional desire for Sophie. The *eros-thanatos* equation is more directly revealed in this book than we are accustomed to find outside the terrain of pornographic material; quite simply, Stingo/Styron is invigorated and sexually stimulated by thoughts of death (other people's, of course, and specifically the death of women). First there is Maria, but she, being irrevocably dead and buried, is quickly eclipsed by something even better—Sophie, the living dead:

While it was a beautiful body, with all the right promi-
nences, curves, continuities and symmetries, there was
something a little strange about it—nothing visibly missing and not so much deficient as reassembled. And that
was precisely it, I could see. The odd quality proclaimed
itself through the skin. It possessed the sickish plasticity
(at the back of the arms it was especially noticeable) of
one who has suffered severe emaciation and whose flesh
is even now in the last stage of being restored.[18]

On one memorable occasion, Stingo walks into Sophie's room
unawares, covertly admiring her 'lustrous blond tresses'. She turns,
startled by a sound, and 'I beheld—for a mercifully fleeting
instant—an old hag whose entire lower face had crumpled in upon
itself, leaving a mouth like a wrinkled gash and an expression of
doddering senescence'.[19] Sophie, it transpires, has left her false
teeth out; but, oh, the rapture with which Stingo dwells upon this
death's head apparition ('It was a mask, withered and pitiable').

A triumphant, all-conquering necrophilia is not the only
sexual fantasy given free rein in the book. Sophie is a cipher, a
creature so consumed by her sense of guilt that she has renounced
all claim to autonomy, given up the right to protest on her own
behalf, no matter what is done to her; her passivity, her absence
of will, call to mind the heroine of the French pornographic
novel, *The Story of O*. And what a lot *is* done to Sophie. Lesbian
rape in the camp, a sexual assault on the subway by a man who
rams a finger into her vagina, and bone-breaking beatings handed
out by Nathan, who taunts her by calling her by the name of Irma
Griese, the notorious concentration-camp guard. We learn that
Nathan has even, long before their suicide pact (if that is what
it is), tried to kill her. In spite of this, in spite of his kicking her
several times in the ribs, she is able to tell Stingo:

'Don't ask me, Stingo, don't ask me why—after all this—I was still ready for Nathan to piss on me, rape me, stab me, beat me, blind me, do anything with me that he desired. Anyway, a long time passed before he spoke to me again. Then he said, "Sophielove [sic], I'm insane, you know. I want to apologize for my insanity." And after a bit he said, "Want to fuck?" And I said right away without even thinking twice, "Yes. Oh yes." And we made love all afternoon . . .'[20]

But Sophie is not merely passive to the point of self-destruction. The fact of her 'guilt'—because of her attempt to save her son at the cost of her daughter, and because of her temporary espousal of anti-Semitism—is central to the narrative; her patient acceptance of violence implies her tacit acknowledgement that these batterings are only what she deserves, and gives Styron carte blanche to do what he likes with her. This combination of suffering and guilt, this perception of Sophie as victim and *collaborateuse*, is an irresistible one, as Stingo/Styron makes clear:

If Sophie had been just a victim . . . she would have seemed merely pathetic, another wretched waif of the storm cast up in Brooklyn with no secrets which had to be unlocked. But the fact of the matter is that at Auschwitz . . . she had been a victim, yes, but both victim and accomplice . . . to the mass slaughter whose sickening vaporous residue spiraled skyward from the chimneys at Birkenau whenever she peered out across the autumnal meadows . . .[21]

Unresisting woman, guilty woman, *punishable* woman: is this really a loving tribute to a long-lost friend? The parallel insistently called to mind while reading *Sophie's Choice* is de Sade's *Justine, or The Misfortunes of Virtue*, in which the heroine, a beautiful woman like Sophie, continually falls into the hands of people who rape, beat or otherwise mistreat her. Angela Carter, in her book *The Sadeian Woman*, offers a description of Justine which could equally well apply to Sophie:

> . . . she is the heroine of a black, inverted fairy-tale and its subject is the misfortunes of unfreedom; Justine embarks on a dolorous pilgrimage in which each proffered sanctuary turns out to be a new prison and all the human relations offered her are a form of servitude.[22]

Critical reactions to *Sophie's Choice* have ranged from the reverential to the ecstatic. That this is so is not unconnected with Styron's past, his reputation as a liberal Southerner and opponent of the Vietnam war. Such credentials have the effect of disarming critics in advance, predisposing them to look kindly on material which might be considered in dubious taste if it emanated from the pen of a less reputable author. The response to another novel which explicitly links sex and the Holocaust, *The White Hotel* by the British author D. M. Thomas, was similarly coloured by Thomas's standing as a poet and supporter of liberal causes.

*The White Hotel* was published in Britain in 1981 to a lukewarm critical reception. But when the American edition was greeted with an hysterical parade of superlatives ('indescribable poetic effect . . . heart-stunning', *The New York Times*), English critics rushed to catch up. The novel is, again, an uneasy mixture of fiction and fact, containing genuine letters from Freud and some made up on his behalf by Thomas. Its genesis alone is enough to sound a warning: Thomas wrote an erotic poem, entitled 'The Woman to Sigmund Freud', which is a fairly transparent attempt to place a masculine model of female sexuality into a woman's mouth. The narrator of the poem, the fictional Anna G, is one of Freud's patients, and the verses are 'her' account of a long erotic fantasy she has constructed about an affair with the psychoanalyst's son. The striking thing about the poem is Anna G's joyfully masochistic response—reminiscent of Styron's heroine in *Sophie's Choice*—to the violent love-making of Freud's son, and the images of death and disaster which accompany their couplings. (It was my intention at this point to quote a passage which illustrates my argument, but, permission to do so having been refused by Thomas's publisher, Gollancz, I regret to say that readers unfamiliar with the book will have either to accept my word or risk exposing themselves to the full blast of his distasteful verses by looking up *The White Hotel* in the nearest public library.) Some time after writing the poem, Thomas later explained in *The London Magazine*, he happened to read an account of a Nazi massacre:

> It was only when I read Kuznetsov's *Babi Yar* that it clicked and I suddenly realized that the poems were, in fact, beginning a novel which would end in *Babi Yar*.[23]

And this is the point of the book: Anna G's erotic fantasies, her passivity, and the way in which her sexual response is associated with, even stimulated by, images of violent death, lead Freud to his second great discovery (he has already articulated the pleasure principle)—the death instinct. As Susanne Kappeler remarks in her essay 'The White Brothel':

> It was only when he read the account of one of history's most violent massacres, abounding in gratuitous brutal-

ity, that [Thomas] saw an 'end' to which his pornographic poems could lead.[24]

Anna G, who is eventually revealed in the novel to be an
opera singer called Lisa Erdman, obligingly arranges the rest of
her life in such a way that she is herded into the ravine with
thousands of other victims at Babi Yar. She is luckless enough
to survive the hail of bullets, and begs a couple of soldiers to
finish her off. Instead, one of them, Demidenko, rapes her. Then,
in a horrifying passage from which I am once again forbidden
to quote, Demidenko tires of the sexual act: complaining of Lisa's
unattractiveness, he withdraws and picks up his rifle. The two
men insert the bayonet into Lisa's vagina and Demidenko uses it
as a substitute penis. His companion laughs loudly as Lisa's body
moves in a parody of intercourse.

There we have it: sex-as-death, the one thing that women
really desire, and Lisa, like Sophie, is fortunate enough to have
men on hand who are ready to give it to her. But there is another
way of looking at *The White Hotel* and at *Sophie's Choice*. The
model of female sexuality constructed by Thomas and Styron has
nothing to do with real women but exists to legitimize masculine
sexual fantasies which are violent, vicious and ultimately lethal.
The rapturous reception of their books, and their status as bestsell-
ers, suggest that a significant proportion of the reading public is
receptive to such fevered imaginings.

1 David Caute, *Sixty-Eight: The Year of the Barricades*, Hamish Hamilton
   1988, p. 139 (Harper & Row, 1988).
2 William Styron, *Sophie's Choice*, Corgi, 1981, p. 197 (Random House,
   1980).

3  Primo Levi, *If This Is A Man* and *The Truce*, introduction by Paul Bailey, Abacus, 1987, p. 11.

4  Styron, op. cit., p. 167.

5  Ibid., see pp. 163–76 and pp. 222–43.

6  Ibid., p. 163.

7  Ibid., p. 575.

8  Ibid., p. 576.

9  Ibid., p. 576.

10  Ibid., p. 241.

11  Ibid., p. 289.

12  Ibid., pp. 66–7.

13  Ibid., p. 657.

14  Ibid., p. 662.

15  Ibid., p. 64.

16  Ibid., p. 66.

17  Ibid., pp. 75–6.

18  Ibid., p. 73.

19  Ibid., p. 178.

20  Ibid., p. 461.

21  Ibid., p. 293.

22  Angela Carter, *The Sadeian Woman*, Virago, 1979, p. 39 (Pantheon, 1988).

23  Quoted in Susanne Kappeler, 'The White Brothel: The Literary Exoneration of the Pornographic', from *Sexuality, A Reader*, edited by *Feminist Review*, Virago, 1987, p. 330.

24  Ibid., Kappeler, p. 330.

# A VISIT FROM THE GAS MAN

## *A play in one act*

*Scene:*   a house in Steeple Aston

*Time:*   a morning in February

*Persons:*   JOAN S., a writer
FRANCIS W., another writer
MR P., a representative of the gas board

(*A doorbell rings*. FRANCIS W. *crosses the hall, opens the door*.)

MR P.: Good morning, you're Mr W.? (FRANCIS W. *nods*) I'm P. from the gas board. I'm here to do a survey, see where we can put the pipes from the main into your house. Won't take very long.

FRANCIS W.: Oh yes, come in. (*Leads the way across the hall into a large kitchen with a Rayburn under the window*) This is Joan S., who also lives here.

JOAN S.: Hello.

MR P.: (*Ignores her*) Oh dear, these quarry tiles will have to come up, make a bit of a mess, that will.

JOAN S.: (*Alarmed*) But they've only just been laid! Isn't there some other way—

MR. P.: (*Ignores her*) Oh, you don't like that idea then, Mr W.? Well, let's leave that for a moment and have a look in here. (*Pokes head into room off kitchen*) Oh dear, oh dear. These paving stones'll have to come up as well . . .

JOAN S.: But you can't take those up! We'd never get them flat again. There must be something else . . .

MR. P.: (*Ignores her*) So you don't like that idea either, Mr W.?

FRANCIS W.: Well, Joan was just saying that she didn't think it was a good idea, and I must say I agree with her.

JOAN S.: Haven't you got some sort of tunnelling device for going under buildings? A mole, I think it's called. Couldn't you use that?

MR P.: (*Ignores her*) We don't use that for domestic installations, Mr W. If you want gas these floors will just have to come up.

JOAN S.: What about putting the pipes above the ceilings? That would be better than taking up the floor.

MR. P.: (*Ignores her*) You don't want to do that, Mr W., you'd have to have the carpets up to do that.

JOAN S.: We'd rather have a few carpets up than the floors.

FRANCIS W.: Joan's right, we'd much rather do it that way.

MR P.: (*Disbelieving*) Well, I suppose if you insist . . .

JOAN S.: Look, we'd rather do it that way, all right?

MR P.: (*Ignores her*) OK, Mr W., have it your way. I'll just take a few measurements . . . (*produces tape measure and scribbles a few notes on a clipboard*) OK, Mr W., that's all I need. (*Crosses kitchen to hall*) Right, I won't trouble you any further. (*Opens front door*) Bye, Mr W. (*Pulls door shut behind him*)


THE END

# CRAWLING FROM
# THE WRECKAGE

You have to pity the poor USAF bomber pilot. There he is in his flying suit, his reflecting aviator glasses, and his multi-million dollar machine, all dressed up and nowhere to go. Until nuclear war breaks out, he is condemned to fly on endless manoeuvres in which he is forbidden to do the very thing he's trained for: kill people. Sorties like the one against Libya in 1986 are, for political reasons, pretty rare. Meanwhile, all he has to do is wait; wait, think, and dream. Sometimes he is moved to write down his dreams, as did a group of pilots from the USAF 77th Tactical Fighter Squadron stationed at Upper Heyford in Oxfordshire. They published their work in the form of a pamphlet called the *Gamblers' Song Book*, named for the squadron's nickname. The introduction, which ends with a quotation from the German First World War flying ace, the Red Baron, reads:

> This book is our thoughts, our songs and our games. Lesser individuals who have never strapped their asses to a piece of flaming metal will consider these of little or no redeeming social value. Because of this, the songs contained in this book are held as sacred by those of us who have. These people do not know, nor will they ever know, what it means to be a FIGHTER PILOT. The book is not for them . . . it is for us. The GAMBLERS is a collection of over 75 years of tradition. A tradition that will never

die as long as enemy aggression challenges for supremacy
of the skies and free men rise to defeat them. 'Anything
else is rubbish.'[1]

The first thing to note is that these are essentially the *private*
thoughts of American pilots; far from being a public relations
exercise, this is what they really think. (The fact that the book
was on sale at an open day at Upper Heyford in 1987 was later
described by the US Air Force as a mistake.) It is clear from the
introduction that the men who compiled it, all pilots of F1-11
nuclear fighter-bombers, consider themselves an elite, the inheri-
tors of an honourable tradition which is unlikely to be understood by 'lesser' individuals, people who are differentiated from
the authors by their implied cowardice and inaction. The songs
in the book are 'sacred'—set apart, entitled to veneration, dedicated to something which is not defined but which is clearly
connected to the defence of the skies by 'free men' against 'enemy
aggression'. For the pilots, then, they are the songs of freedom.
What do they tell us about their preoccupations?

The tone is set by the squadron's theme tune, 'Heyford's Own
Victor Alert Song',[2] which was written to be sung to 'My
Favourite Things' from *The Sound of Music* . The first verse reads:

> Reading our porno and picking our asses
> Checking our forms out and passing our gasses
> Silver sleek B-61's slung below
> Nuclear war and we're ready to go.

The pilots' two main concerns, sex and war, are instantly
revealed; the first activity occupies their time, even in the vicari-
ous form of reading pornography, until the second takes over.

Sex and death form a continuum. A couple of verses later, the enemy is identified:

> Leaving the orbit our pits start to sweat
> We'll asshole those fuckers and that's a sure bet
> Burn all those Ruskies [sic] and cover 'em with dirt
> That's why we love sitting Victor Alert.

The sexual imagery now carries over into combat itself: the Russians, 'those fuckers', will be 'assholed' in turn; here the enemy's preoccupation with sex, far from being an admirable trait as it is in the American pilots, is a sign of his degeneracy and will be punished by the humiliation of buggery. (The very next stanza opens with the aside that thinking about 'fagots' [sic] 'scares the shit out of me'.) The song's final verse and chorus are as follows:

> Nearing the target, our nerves they are STEADY
> Switches are thrown and we got us a READY
> Bay doors are open, the jobs [sic] almost done
> Killing those Commies, we're having some fun
>
> When the shit fills up your flight suit
> And you're feeling had, just simply remember that
> Big mushroom cloud, and then you won't feel so BAD.

The sexual imagery persists in the form of an undertone: the ambiguous phrase 'we got us a READY' could apply equally to a state of preparedness for sex or for war. The chorus is similarly ambiguous. The pilot, suddenly overwhelmed by terror, is exhorted to remember that 'Big mushroom cloud', the after-effect

of detonation which, streaming unstoppably upwards and out-
wards, could well stand as a metaphor for orgasm. But the song
expresses above all else a powerful mixture of bravado in the face
of the enemy, and fear. The paradox of these men's existence is
that the job they are trained to do—dropping nuclear bombs on
the enemy, who is variously described as the 'Commies', 'Persian-
pukes' and, in the older songs, the 'Viet Cong'—is likely to cost
them their lives. They exist in a state of anticipation, fuelled by
simplistic right-wing politics, in which the longed-for event is
also the final mission: what they are waiting for, longing for,
dreaming of, is death. It is hardly surprising, then, that death—
violent death—haunts the fifty-two pages of the book; yet it is
also the case that the enemy who is the probable instrument of
their own destruction is dealt with in an almost perfunctory way.
The song 'Phantom Flyers in the Sky'[3] stands out from the rest
of the book in that the notional enemy *is* addressed, and addressed
directly, in its three short verses; its loathing of the Muslims, and
in particular the Iranians, suggests it is a response to a specific
event, the holding of hostages in the American embassy in Teh-
ran. The first stanza runs:

> Phantom flyers in the sky,
> Persian-pukes prepare to die,
> Rolling in with snake and nape,
> Allah creates but we cremate.

The emotions behind the lyric, crude racism and a thirst for
revenge, are relatively uncomplicated. Not so those which inspire
the bulk of the songs in the book. They tend, as I said before,
to be on the subjects of sex or death or, more often, sex-and-
death. More specifically, they are about women and death. Time
and time again, woman is the image chosen to represent death,

as in the following song whose tune will immediately be evident from its title, 'Ghost Fuckers in the Sky':[4]

> An old cowpoke went riding out
> One dark and windy day
> Stopped beneath a shady tree
> And paused to beat his meat
> When all at once a slant-eyed bitch
> Came ridin' down the trail
> He stopped her and asked her
> How 'bout a piece of tail?
>
> Her tits were all a floppin'
> Her cunt ate out with clap
> He socked it to her anyway
> And gave her ass a slap
> She shit, she moaned
> She groaned
> She threw him from her crack
> He rolled across the desert
> And broke his fucking back.

The song describes exactly the state of the F1-11 pilot's psyche as he sets off on the final mission: at long last (he is an 'old cowpoke', he has been waiting for this) he sees the enemy, who both allures and repels him ('a slant-eyed bitch came ridin' down the trail'), sees his own death embodied there ('Her cunt ate out with clap'), but his desire, fuelled by years of self-denial, is too strong ('He socked it to her anyway'). The attack, which is visualized as a rape, results in his own death ('broke his fucking back'). The song is fatalistic; the protagonist unquestioningly accepts his fate.

This is not the case throughout the book. The most extraordinary and disturbing song in it is baldly entitled 'I Fucked a Dead Whore';[5] it runs as follows:

> I fucked a dead whore by the road side,
> I knew right away she was dead.
> The skin was all gone from her tummy,
> The hair was all gone from her head.
>
> And as I lay down there beside her,
> I knew right away that I had sinned.
> So I pressed my lips to her sweet pussy,
> And sucked out the wad I'd shot in.
>
> Sucked out, sucked out,
> I sucked out the wad I'd shot in, shot in,
> Sucked out, sucked out,
> I sucked out the wad I'd shot in.

These lines, which bring irresistibly to mind the crimes of the Yorkshire Ripper, are very different in tone from 'Ghost Fuckers in the Sky'. Here, far from acquiescing in his own destruction, the protagonist triumphantly cheats death. He begins by willingly involving himself with it ('I knew right away she was dead'), even revelling in the manifestations of decay, yet refuses to pay the price of the encounter ('I knew right away that I had sinned'), withdrawing not only himself but his life force—his sperm. It is a fantasy in which the pilot goes into battle, experiences the sexual thrill of killing, *and still manages to escape with his life*. Both songs raise the question of what the pilots see in a woman that leads them to use her as their chief image for death.

One clue lies in the way in which women's bodies appear to

provoke both excitement and disgust in the pilots. Even in the song just quoted, the corpse's 'pussy' is sweet, and the act of retrieving his sperm provides the protagonist with an opportunity for the covert performance of a sexual act—cunnilingus—which is often construed as humiliating for men. (The song also hints at the breaking of an even greater taboo, that of homosexuality; when the protagonist sucks back his sperm from the corpse, his part in the proceeding is analogous to that of the passive partner in the act of fellatio.) Other songs in the book are straightforward tirades directed at women's bodies in which no attempt is made to disguise the contempt the pilots feel for them, and particularly for their sexuality. The intense loathing which inspires a song called 'These Foolish Things (Remind Me Of You)'[6] makes this point crystal clear:

> Ten pounds of tittie in a loose brassiere,
> A twat that twitches like a mouses [sic] ear,
> Ejaculation in my glass of beer
> These foolish things remind me of you.

> A pubic hair upon my breakfast roll,
> A bloody Kotex in my toilet bowl,
> The smelly fragrance of your fat asshole,
> These foolish things remind me of you.

> A sloppy blowjob in a taxicab,
> A cunt that's covered with syphilitic scabs,
> These foolish things remind me of you.

In this song, as in some of the others mentioned above, the protagonist feels a powerful and confusing blend of attraction and repulsion for the woman he is addressing. He simultaneously desires and despises both the manifestations of her sex and the feelings she provokes in him. Because the desire is strong, it seems unlikely that the woman's vagina really is 'covered with syphilitic scabs'; this is a *wish* on the pilot's part, the punishment he would like to impose on her, not a description of what he can actually see. A similar image crops up in 'The Ballad of Lupe',[7] a song about a Mexican prostitute, but is this time taken further. The woman Lupe is praised at the beginning of the song for her skill at fellatio, only to wind up 'dead in her tomb, while maggots crawl out of her decomposed womb' at the end. This is an important indicator of what is going on in the pilots' minds: here death and decomposition are the woman's punishment for the *pleasurable* feelings she has stirred up in the protagonist. It is not a huge step from wanting women dead, thinking that they deserve to die, to appropriating them as an image for death itself. But not just for death; although the transformation is never directly acknowledged, women fulfil a further role for the pilots in that they take the place of the distant, unseen, and unknowable enemy. Indeed, it is clear from the songs that in some sense women *are* the enemy.

Why should American pilots regard women as the real enemy? The US is often described as a matriarchal society, whatever that means, and it would be possible to construct an answer to the question which used that classification—the idea that the men's loathing is a response to a particular sort of power structure—as a starting-point. Such an answer would, however, be specific to one time and place, obscuring the fact that we are dealing with a phenomenon which has been observed in other, unrelated military units. Klaus Theweleit, a German academic, has studied the literature of the *Freikorps*, the private right-wing death squads which roamed Germany after the First World War, many of whose members were later recruited by the Nazis. (Rudolf Höss, commandant of Auschwitz, was a member of the *Freikorps* commanded by a man called Gerhard Rossbach and was sent to prison for five years for murder in 1923.) In his book about members of the *Freikorps, Male Fantasies*,[8] Theweleit examines a mass of material including their novels and autobiographies. There are obvious differences between these writings and the Upper Heyford songs; for one thing, the *Freikorps* literature is much greater in volume than our little songbook. For another, most of the German material was written specifically for publication, for propaganda purposes, and its sexual content is correspondingly circumscribed by its wider market. Nevertheless, we still find passages of sexual sadism in which women undergo humiliation as a punishment for their supposed sexual activities in a manner reminiscent of the 'whores' in the USAF songbook. *Riders in the German Night* by Hanns Heinz Ewers (1932) is a long, complicated novel whose *Freikorps* hero, First Lieutenant Gerhard Scholz, is incestuously loved by his sister, Käte. In order to save Scholz from prison, Käte gives herself to a Belgian colonel and gains a reputation as a whore. She is captured by a group of German youths, admirers of Scholz, who put her on trial, cut off her hair, force her to take a laxative, and march her off into the woods:

> 'Jump to it, sweetheart,' their leader says. 'You'll find a pig's wallow down there—the sort of place a prize slut like you belongs!'
> She stood there on the country road, helpless, immobile.
> 'Get a move on, fairy princess!' the leader warned. 'Into the woods with you. A bit of movement will soon

warm you up. A sight for sore eyes, you are—with your bald head and shit all over your dress!' The other boy gave her a whack across her fanny with his switch. 'Move it, you whore, before I have to do it for you!'

She turned around and felt a second lash across her left breast. The pain bit into her. She let out a shrill scream.[9]

Käte's captors leave her to wander through the woods, too ashamed of her condition to approach anyone and ask for help. Eventually she dies of pneumonia. There is a striking parallel between Käte the 'whore', bald and shit-smeared, and the 'dead whore' whom the USAF airman found by the roadside. Each woman is punished for her sexuality—the whore for being a whore (how did he know that's what she was, by the way? Because *all* women are whores?), Käte because of her incestuous passion and her relationship with the Belgian colonel, even though the purpose of the latter was her brother's freedom. Scholz himself understands this perfectly: in Theweleit's words, 'he finds the lads' action above reproach; indeed he commissions his own attorney to take over the defence of his sister's murderers'.

What the *Freikorps* writings lack in descriptions of sex they make up for in those of violence. At first glance this differentiates them from the USAF songs, in which women tend to be already dead when the action begins or progress to that state without obvious violence; one explanation for this is that the *Freikorps* men were seasoned fighters, familiar with cavalry charges and street battles in a way that airmen, engaging in combat only at long distance, are not (this is particularly true of the Upper Heyford pilots, few of whom have ever been in action). Favourite targets for the *Freikorps* fighters are the Red Army rifle-women, fantasy monsters who, according to E. F. Berendt's National Socialist Primer, a propaganda publication from 1935, 'were the sort of cruel furies only Bolshevism could devise. While the heart of one of the men of the Red Army might be moved to pity at the sight of suffering innocents, those women were bestialized and devoid of all human feelings.'[10] In other words, we are back with the idea that, no matter who the ostensible enemy might be, women always constitute the group who are most to be feared. Theweleit quotes a passage from Edwin Dwinger's novel *Die letzten Reiter* ('The Last Riders', 1935) in which one of these Red Army women, Marja, falls into *Freikorps* hands and is murdered by assassins hired by the hero, Pahlen:

Pahlen pulls out a wallet that still gleams with the imprint of a seven-pointed crown, its edges worn smooth with use, and hands them a large bill. 'There's nothing to be afraid of. It's not against orders. She's murdered so many people that this is simply a punishment for her crimes.'

'A rifle-woman then?' the first one asks.

'A genuine rifle-woman!' Pahlen nods absent-mindedly.

The first man nods and licks his lips. 'Then everything's in order. We'd have done it even without the bill. One of the famous rifle-women, is she?' He repeats, shaking his head as he stares at her. Then they bend down again, grab her by her shattered arms, and haul her brutally away. Pahlen takes one look at her face; she seems fully conscious, yet it is distorted by an animal hatred. Curses spring from her protruding lips, pouring forth with every breath she takes.[11]

A few minutes later, Pahlen's squadron moves off. He passes a stream packed with the bodies of dead Bolsheviks:

> The last body they ride past seems to be that of a woman. But it's very hard to tell, since all that's been left is a bloody mass, a lump of flesh that appears to have been completely lacerated with whips and is now lying within a circle of trampled, reddish slush.[12]

Although Pahlen has not witnessed the killing himself, he relives it vicariously in this passage—first the whipping, then the trampling into 'reddish slush'. In another Dwinger novel, *Auf halbem Wege* ('Only Half Way', 1939), his *Freikorps* hero Donat is confronted by a mob of shouting, howling women and shoots one of them:

> Everything turns suddenly to frenzied flight. Yet Donat sees nothing of this. He sees only the woman who was standing there before him a moment ago. It threw her onto her back, as if she had been blown over by some gigantic wind. Is that thing at his feet really her? That person without a face? The head isn't really a head anymore, just a monstrous, bloody throat. 'I warned her,' Donat thinks to himself, trembling. 'I warned her . . .'[13]

The *Freikorps* men's attempts to justify their attacks on women have a subtle parallel in the Upper Heyford songbook. Here we find an emphasis not on women's guilt in being allied with the actual enemy (and in being even more barbarous than he happens to be), but on their sexual infidelity and their proclivity to use up men. Several of the songs about sexually active women warn of their insatiability: 'she'll suck out your guts'. In

a song called 'No Balls At All',[14] the theme is female conspiracy;
a woman who has married a man 'with a very short peter and
no balls at all' bemoans her husband's sexual incapacity to her
mother and is advised to take lovers. The result is a bouncing
baby foisted on the cuckolded husband. 'Masturbating Man',[15] a
complaint about the untrustworthiness of women, begins with
the line:

> Melinda was mine, til [sic] the time that I found her,
> sucking Jim, blowing him.

The song ends with the protagonist's averral that:

>         . . . until I can find me,
> A girl who'll lay and won't play games behind me,
> I'll be what I am a Masturbating Man.

These complaints have a manufactured air, just as do the
*Freikorps* fantasies about wild-eyed, barbarous rifle-women; we
are still faced with the question of why these diverse groups of
military men should detest women to so great a degree and take
pleasure in their destruction. Klaus Theweleit's perceptive observation about the *Freikorps* men seems equally true of both groups:

> The women's crime seems to be that they excite the men
> too much and that the men cannot stand this inner tur-
> moil.[16]

He backs it up with a revealing passage from *Der Berg der
Rebellen* ('The Mountain of the Rebels', 1937) by Kurt Eggers:

> With their screams and filthy giggling, vulgar women
> excite men's urges.

Let our revulsion flow into a single river of destruction. A destruction which will be incomplete if it does
not also trample their hearts and souls.[17]

Military men, probably more than any others, spend their
lives in a state of repressed emotion. Normal human reactions to
dangerous situations must be kept at bay if they are to carry out
their function. Women pose a particular threat, since love and
affection could force a chink in the men's armour which would
then allow in unwanted feelings—fear and the urge to flee instead
of fight. (The characters in some *Freikorps* novels boast openly
of their imperviousness to female charms.) But this is not in itself
the whole answer. It is clear that the men are also afraid of
women's sexuality, both because it disgusts them and because they
cannot cope with the intense feelings it arouses in them. The
reaction is partly explained by the fact that most Judaeo-Christian
societies hate sex, and the men in them have inherited a tradition
which projects on to women the bad feelings that accompany
their own arousal. By obliterating the women they hope to avoid
having the feelings in the future; that is why Eggers, in the
passage quoted above, is determined that the annihilation of
women should be complete, that it should 'trample their hearts
and souls'—vague terms which nevertheless refer to the repressed
feelings and sensibility which, in a curious reversal, the women
are seen to have projected on to the men rather than the other
way round. But the fear of women expressed by both sets of men
is so overwhelming that it cannot simply be sexual, and I think
the final answer is this: men who are part of a macho, swaggering
culture, as are the USAF pilots at Upper Heyford and as were
the proto-Nazis of the *Freikorps*, have placed themselves in a
position where they constantly have to prove their masculine
identity. A key element of this identity is their distance, their

separateness, from women. One of the characteristics that differentiates them from the other sex is their prized absence of feeling (men who *do* feel emotion are dismissed as sissies). Having thus built up their defences, they are unused to coping with intense urges or desires. When they are suddenly caught unawares, whether by love or lust or pity or rage, they have no experience to fall back on, nothing to guide them or tell them how to cope. They are swept back helplessly to the one period in their lives when the barricades against emotion were still down, the earliest days of their existence when they were in a close symbiotic relationship with their mothers. That is a lost paradise: no matter how happy they were at that time, nestled in women's arms and reliant on them for affection and sustenance, they have since learned to despise themselves for their involuntary acquiescence to female power and for their 'feminine' acceptance of feeling. Even worse, it was a time when they lacked the vaunted masculine identity, when they were half merged with the female, not knowing the boundary between their fledgeling selves and their mothers' accommodating bodies. Now, as outwardly tough but secretly vulnerable adult men, their greatest fear is a return to that humiliating state, a return which threatens every time they are confronted by intense feeling. For them, emotion is truly overwhelming, a threat to their carefully constructed masculine existence; is it surprising that the dreams of such men are dreams of dead women?

1 *Gamblers' Song Book*, USAF 77th Tactical Fighter Squadron, Upper Heyford, Oxon; compiled by Capt. George 'Kelmaniac' Kelman, Capt. Thomas 'Tunes' Theobald, Capt. Mike 'Boomer' Clowers, Capt. Tom 'Grunt' Carmichael, SRA John 'The Kid' Galletta.
2 Ibid., p. 1.
3 Ibid., p. 30.

 4  Ibid., p. 21.
 5  Ibid., p. 13.
 6  Ibid., p. 32.
 7  Ibid., p. 14.
 8  Klaus Theweleit, *Male Fantasies*, Polity Press, 1987 (Univ. of Minnesota Press, 1987).
 9  Ibid., p. 119.
10  Ibid., p. 76.
11  Ibid., p. 188.
12  Ibid., p. 189.
13  Ibid., pp. 179–80.
14  *Gamblers' Song Book*, p. 7.
15  Ibid., p. 27.
16  Theweleit, op. cit., p. 180.
17  Ibid., p. 180.

# PRIMA
# DONNA

Mrs Thatcher striding across a stage for a press conference; Mrs Thatcher getting off an aeroplane during a foreign trip; Mrs Thatcher picking up litter in a carefully staged appearance in a London park; Mrs Thatcher taking her place in a group photograph of world leaders; Mrs Thatcher hurrying across a piece of waste land in an anonymous inner city; the least conspicuous yet most significant thing about all these images is the handbag that perpetually swung from the Prime Minister's left arm. It was her totem, her badge, the object that marked her out. The rest of her appearance—the perennial suit, the discreet blouse, the plain though high-heeled shoes—was no more than an adaptation of male uniform, the formal clothing worn by the men who trailed in her wake, the Parkinsons, Lawsons, Howes and Bakers who made up her entourage. She was of them and not of them, one of the boys as long as it benefited her, but she always kept in reserve the fact of her sex, her essential difference: her gender was unobtrusive, just like her handbag, but eternally set her apart.

Mrs Thatcher was not just another British prime minister, one in a long line stretching back for hundreds of years; she was the first woman to do the job. This fact, this singular achievement, is used time and time again in answer to women who complain about the discrimination they suffer in their everyday lives. If Mrs Thatcher could do it, the argument runs, so could anyone else. The unspoken implication is that the woman making the complaint simply has not tried hard enough, or has wasted valuable time bemoaning her lot instead of emulating the Right Hon lady. Sometimes the argument is taken even further: Mrs Thatcher's lengthy occupancy of 10 Downing Street is adduced as evidence not only that unparalleled opportunities are open to women, if they have the sense to grasp them, but that there is now a definite *advantage* in being a woman.

The latter is true only in a strictly limited sense; very often the people who claim to utilize positive discrimination do so for entirely the wrong reasons, such as preferring a female reception- ist because male clients like to see a pretty face when they arrive for a business appointment. Or, as the manager of a DHSS office remarked, when interviewing me for a job during a university vacation, because 'women are better at boring jobs'. (He seemed surprised when I didn't take it.) Wider opportunities for some women there certainly are, but that has very little to do with Mrs Thatcher; indeed her employment and economic policies, which limited access to work for millions of people, reduced the number of jobs available to women, not increased it.

But to discuss Mrs Thatcher in terms of a positive meaning for women is a mistake; there isn't one. (The writer Eileen Fairweather once remarked that Mrs Thatcher might be a woman, but she certainly wasn't a sister.) Her success lay in her ability to perform a trick, one which was both clever and success- ful but nevertheless dishonest, and it was this: to all intents and purposes, Mrs Thatcher disguised herself as a man. But, and it is an important but, she never renounced her right to claim the privileges of a woman. Hence her handbag, symbol that, no matter how tough and ambitious a political animal she might be (like Michael Heseltine, the man who engineered her downfall), no matter how much she shared the political ideas of her close associates (particularly Nicholas Ridley and Lord Young), there was always something that differentiated her from them. To goad her was a risk; she never accepted the boundaries which men, particularly men with the background shared by most members of her Cabinet, observe by tacit agreement as a means of protecting themselves from each other. They know when to stop (or, at least, they recognize when they have overstepped the mark and act accordingly, as Heseltine did when he left the Cabinet during the Westland affair); she had recourse to temper when argument failed, to emotion—to the *unpredictability* that is said to be the hallmark of feminine behaviour. She had a foot in both camps, shamelessly combining 'masculine' ruthlessness with 'feminine' bossiness: 'I don't mind how much my ministers talk—as long as they do what I say',[1] she once remarked.

Her covert adherence to a traditional model of femininity was most marked when it came to her attitude to the rest of her sex, an attitude which was competitive and owed nothing to any notion of female solidarity. She insisted: 'I owe nothing to women's lib'.[2] The election of Britain's first female prime minister, far from leading to an increase in the proportion of women achieving Cabinet status, actually kept women away from the higher echelons of government—so much so that her successor, John Major, was able to fall back on the excuse of a shortage of experienced female politicians when challenged over his failure to include a single woman in his first Cabinet. Mrs Thatcher's success was built on other women's failure, and she had a vested interest in keeping them in their place. No *prima inter pares* for her; she was prima donna of British politics, the woman who revelled in being unique.

This was not the image she projected in public; it was characteristic of her tendency to disguise and dissimulation that, in an interview in 1988, she should express her disappointment with the number of women holding important jobs, complaining that: 'It makes those of us who *are* in public life more conspicuous than we ought to be'.[3] From someone who missed no chance to be photographed with other leaders, who played up to her soubriquet, the Iron Lady, with an enthusiasm which gained her a position of undeserved prominence on the world stage, the claim is conspicuously disingenuous. But there is a deeper dishonesty here. Throughout the interview, Mrs Thatcher presented herself as an example of what a woman can achieve if she is determined to combine work and family: 'I am constantly saying to women who want to go out to work, please, when you are married and have children you will [*sic*] always be able to make some arrangement to keep in touch with your skill. Whether it is in journalism, whether it is being able to do beautiful things in craft, if you are a technical person working in a laboratory, *keep in touch* . . . You simply can never deny the fundamental relationship between mother and child, nor should you. But I am constantly saying it is possible to do both'.

It was exhortations of this kind which allowed Mrs Thatcher's supporters to cite her as an example for other women. But what Mrs Thatcher rarely talked about is just how she went about putting her own advice into practice. 'Usually it is possible for a woman to make arrangements for someone who can come and look after the children', was her throwaway remark in the same interview on the subject of combining career and motherhood, making it sound as if the question of child care is simply one of efficient organization. The observation concealed the fact that Mrs Thatcher's entire political career was based upon her status as a kept woman. When she was shown around Parliament for the first time, she made this admission: 'I am very lucky because I have my own secretary. You know, I could only do it on Denis's money'.[4] It is hardly surprising that, as she revealed in the House of Commons in May 1988, she never found it necessary to draw her full prime ministerial salary. Mrs Thatcher was not only the first British woman premier, she was also the first pin-money prime minister. Denis Thatcher, whom she married in 1951 just after she stood unsuccessfully as a Conservative parliamentary candidate for the second time, inherited a family paint and chemicals business. When their twin children arrived in 1953, a live-in nurse was hired immediately after the birth. She was soon replaced by nannies. It was her husband's financial support which allowed Mrs Thatcher to qualify shortly afterwards as a lawyer; her full-time career as a tax barrister lasted only five years, hardly long enough to make the kind of money required to send two children to boarding school (Mark went to Harrow). After her election to Parliament in 1959, her lifestyle—which included a house in fashionable Flood Street, Chelsea, until the couple bought their unused neo-Georgian retirement home in Dulwich—was cushioned by Denis's increasing affluence. The relevance of all this for other ambitious women is simply to demonstrate the undeniable financial rewards concomitant on marrying a wealthy husband, a message no more radical—and of no more practical use to the great mass of women—than the Marilyn Monroe film *How to Marry a Millionaire*. (The habit of relying on rich men is hard to break, as was revealed by Mrs Thatcher's career after leaving office. Contributions to the Thatcher Foundation, her bid for continuing star status, were solicited on her behalf from some of the world's wealthiest men, including a Hong Kong shipping magnate and the Sultan of Brunei.)

It was nothing but the same old trick: Mrs Thatcher pretending to be something she wasn't, whether it was the man among men or the woman among women. In Cabinet she was any other Conservative politician until the moment came when she failed to get her way, whereupon she stamped her foot and reminded her colleagues that underneath it all she was a capricious, bossy female who was quite prepared to beat them about the head with her handbag. In the features pages of newspapers and magazines she was the ordinary working woman, striving to balance the competing demands of family and career, someone who *understood* the conflicts facing working mothers. Here, for once, Mrs Thatcher herself was being used, as a stick with which to beat all those members of the female sex who complain that society makes it virtually impossible to combine children and a job. She did it; why can't they? Even worse, her emphasis on the importance of the home was sometimes the peg on which to hang articles which exhorted women to espouse those Victorian values she herself admired and return to the home ('THATCHER TO WOMEN: Always put your family first'[5]). In this case, though, our houseproud premier seemed to have forgotten that her handbag was stuffed with tenners—and most of them were not hers but her husband's.

1. Jonathon Green, *The Book of Political Quotes,* Angus and Robertson, 1982, p. 149.
2. Ibid, p. 180.
3. Interview with Chris Buckland, *Today,* February 1988.
4. Nicholas Wapshott and George Brock, *Thatcher,* Futura, 1983, p. 59.
5. Headline of *Today* interview with Chris Buckland.

# THERE'S ONLY ONE
# YORKSHIRE RIPPER

The difference between Peter Sutcliffe and Jack the Ripper is the difference between fact and fiction. Unlike Sutcliffe, Jack the Ripper is not a person but a *label* connecting a set of related acts; he has no proper name, no address, no biographical details. The things we 'know' about Jack the Ripper are a mishmash of facts and supposition culled in a haphazard way from the thriving industry which has sprung out of his crimes—dozens of books and films ranging in tone, content and intention from the serious to the sensational, from the mildly dotty to the bizarre, and naming everyone from the Duke of Clarence to Sherlock Holmes as the killer. As fast as each new book appears, proudly 'revealing' the murderer to be the painter Walter Sickert or a previously unknown Polish lunatic, someone else rushes to demolish the theory and replace it with his (my use of the pronoun is intentional) own suspect. The books are an unwitting testament to the one permanent characteristic of Jack the Ripper: his *unknowability*. As I write, exactly 100 years after the Whitechapel murders, it is clear that the odds against anyone ever proving the identity of the murderer are millions and millions to one. (Some would question whether it is important to do so, but that is another matter.) The fact remains that we are ignorant of the killer's name, his occupation, where he lived, his marital status, his habits, even his social class.

And yet, and yet. In the late 1970s, faced with a mass mur-

derer whose death-toll quickly overtook that of the Victorian
killer, police in the north of England embarked on a wild goose
chase for a man they visualized as a reincarnation of Jack the
Ripper. This is the terrible mistake, the appalling blunder, that
lies at the heart of the case; this is the real reason why Peter
William Sutcliffe was able to roam with impunity through the
towns and cities of northern England for more than five years,
restlessly searching out his victims: if you devote your resources
to tracking down a figure from myth, if you waste your time
starting at shadows, you are not likely to come up with a lorry
driver from Bradford.

Sutcliffe was finally picked up on the evening of 2 January
1981, by two uniformed policemen in Sheffield who belonged
not to the West Yorkshire force who had been running the
Ripper inquiry for more than five years but to the South Yorkshire police. He was caught because he made a foolish mistake—
attaching false number plates to his car with black tape. In the
torrent of words that followed his arrest—West Yorkshire police, who had signally failed to catch him, even called a press
conference to crow over his capture—there was a palpable air of
surprise that this calm, unremarkable man had turned out to be
the murderer. Sutcliffe, a married man living in a semi-detached
house in a good suburb of Bradford, was simply not what anyone
had expected. By the time his trial took place, surprise was
turning to anger as the scale of the blunders made by West
Yorkshire police began to emerge. Sutcliffe had been interviewed
not once but *nine* times. He wore the same size boots as the
murderer (indeed, the boot which had left an impression on a
sheet in the flat of one of the victims, and on the thigh of another,
was standing in Sutcliffe's garage as he was interviewed). His only
alibi for the murders was given, contrary to police procedure, by

close relatives, including his wife. He had a previous conviction, dating back to 1973, as a result of being found in a woman's garden with a knife and hammer—the very weapons used by the Ripper. He was one of only 300 men who could have received in his pay packet the brand-new £5 note found in the handbag of one of the Manchester victims, Jean Jordan. His appearance matched fairly closely photofit pictures created by two of his surviving victims. His various cars, which had left tyre prints at the scenes of some of the murders, were frequently logged by police in red-light districts in Bradford, Leeds and Manchester. By an extraordinary coincidence, he had a gap between his front teeth, as the killer was believed to have—even though this clue came from a murder which Sutcliffe *hadn't* committed. Even without being aware of all these facts, an alert detective constable who interviewed Sutcliffe in the summer of 1979 after his Sunbeam Rapier had been seen thirty-six times in Manningham, the red-light district of Bradford, submitted a report suggesting that he should be investigated more thoroughly. He wasn't; his name was never added to the D62 file, the list of 1,000 men who were considered the most likely suspects.

Ronald Gregory, the Chief Constable of the West Yorkshire police force throughout the period of the Ripper murders, later blamed inefficiencies in the organization of the inquiry for his force's failure to catch Sutcliffe:

On four occasions the interviewing officer—or pair of officers, because they usually worked as a team—believed they were questioning Sutcliffe for the first time. Our filing system was in chaos. At times there was a nine-month backlog of reports and statements waiting to be cross-indexed.[1]

There is some truth in this explanation but it does not get anywhere near the heart of the matter, which is this: throughout the hunt for the Yorkshire Ripper, the police forces of several northern counties did little more than stumble about in a fog as dense as that used to invoke the atmosphere of Victorian London in many a film about Jack the Ripper. And, like the pea-soupers which choked the lungs of the inhabitants of the metropolis right up until the 1950s, it was a fog very much of their own making. How did it happen?

When a man (and it usually is a man) murders a number of complete strangers, the police often have very little information on which to base their investigation. They have to rely on forensic evidence, often of a meagre kind, plus sightings of what might be the killer by passers-by or surviving victims. The difficulty of hunting so insubstantial a figure, and the inevitable public pressure for an early arrest, combine to nudge the police in the direction of assigning characteristics to the man they are looking for—to make him into an acquaintance, someone they can talk about as a real person among themselves and to the press. (Two Ripper Squad detectives, interviewed by a newspaper in 1979, described how they and their colleagues discussed the case constantly in their breaks and at the police club bar, referring to the killer as 'Jack', 'the lad', or 'chummy'.[2]) So strong is this impulse to assign an identity to the murderer that, in the 1960s, police in the United States hunting the criminal known as the Boston Strangler brought in a team of doctors and psychiatrists to draw up a psychiatric profile of the man they were looking for. The result was disastrous.[3] The killer, police were told, was a man who hated his mother; each time he dispatched one of his elderly victims, he was ritually slaughtering his loathed mother. Suspects were closely questioned to establish whether they fitted the profile, and eliminated accordingly; the killings went on, then suddenly stopped; eventually a man named Albert DeSalvo, committed to a state mental institution after a series of bizarre burglaries, admitted that he was the murderer. When the key question was put to him, DeSalvo insisted he was very fond of his mother, though he intensely disliked his violent father. The police and the psychiatric team were convinced only when DeSalvo revealed details of the murders which had never been made public. His explanation for selecting elderly victims was pragmatic: they put up less of a fight. Later, as his confidence grew, he had turned to younger women.

The case that quickly became known as the Yorkshire Ripper murders began in the summer of 1975 on the fringes of the sprawling Bradford-Leeds conurbation in the north of England.[4] The sequence began with three attacks in which the victims survived, all in a very short space of time—a period of two months. In the early hours of Saturday 5 July 1975, a woman called Anna Rogulskyj, then thirty-seven, went to the house of her boyfriend, with whom she had quarrelled the previous evening, in Keighley, a small town seven miles north-west of Bradford. She was unable to rouse him, started to walk away from the house and was found, shortly afterwards, lying badly injured in a nearby alley. She had three head wounds which appeared to have been made with a hammer, and slash wounds to her stomach inflicted with a sharp instrument after her clothing had been lifted up. She had not been raped.

In the following month, August 1975, two more assaults took place. One of them involved Olive Smelt, forty-six, who lived in Halifax, eleven miles south of Keighley. One Friday, Mrs Smelt had been out for the evening with friends who dropped her within walking distance of her home after the pubs closed. A man with a local accent came up and spoke to her about the weather; minutes later she was struck on the head. Her injuries included two blows to the head with a hammer or hammer-type instrument, and slash marks on her back. Her clothing had been disarranged. The other attack took place in Silsden, about four miles north of Keighley, the town where Anna Rogulskyj had survived severe head injuries a few weeks before. This time the victim was Tracey Browne, aged fourteen, who also suffered terrible head injuries but was able to give an excellent description of the man who attacked her; the police put together a photofit, which was to bear a remarkable resemblance to that provided by a later surviving victim, Marilyn Moore, *and to Sutcliffe himself*.

A pattern was already emerging. All the victims were women, though they had little else in common, ranging from fourteen to forty-six years of age. Not only was none of the women a prostitute, but one of the attacks took place in a small, leafy town with a river running through the middle of it— Silsden—without a hint of a red-light district. The assaults had taken place in a confined geographical area, and within a short space of time. At least two of them were committed late at night. Each victim received similar, horrific head injuries. In the cases of Mrs Rogulskyj and Mrs Smelt, their clothing had been moved and further wounds inflicted on their torsos. There should have been every reason for police to link the cases, at least tentatively, as the work of the same man, and a man whose motive was an overwhelming hatred of women—any woman. They did not. Nor did they make anything of the fact that two of the women had given them significant clues: Tracey Browne's photofit and— if Mrs Smelt's attacker was the man who spoke to her about the weather moments before she was felled—the likelihood that he had a local accent.

It was not long before the attacker struck again. This time the victim, twenty-eight-year-old Wilma McCann, did not survive. Her body was found just before eight in the morning of

30 October 1975, lying on playing fields in Leeds, twenty or so miles from Keighley and eighteen from Halifax. Mrs McCann was known to the police through minor convictions for drunkenness and theft, and they believed that she sometimes worked as a prostitute, although she had no record for this type of offence. She had been out drinking in several pubs the night before her body was discovered, had been seen by witnesses on her own in the Room at the Top Club, and was last spotted just after one in the morning trying to hitch a lift home; she made a habit of jumping out in front of lorries and demanding that the driver give her a lift. She, too, had head wounds, two of them; she had also been stabbed in the neck and fourteen times in the chest and abdomen after her clothing had been torn open. Traces of semen were found on the back of her trousers.

Less than three months later, in January 1976, the man committed a second murder. This time the victim was Emily Jackson, forty-two, whose body was also found in Leeds. Mrs Jackson had been working as a prostitute for about four weeks because she and her husband were in financial difficulties. She was last seen around seven o'clock in the evening of 20 January; her body was found the next morning. She had extensive hammer injuries to the head and multiple stab wounds to the lower neck, upper chest and abdomen. Her clothing had been disarranged.

It was at this point in the case—not after the three assaults, but when two murders had been committed—that someone thought they'd discerned a pattern. On the very day Mrs Jackson's body was found, West Yorkshire police telexed all their own divisions and neighbouring forces, giving details of Mrs Jackson's murder.[5] She was, it said, an 'active prostitute'; her killer 'may also have been responsible for the death of the prostitute Wilma McCann at Leeds'. The motive, it continued, 'appears to be hatred of prostitutes'. Two days later, the national papers added their own interpretation: a 'Jack the Ripper Killer' was on the loose.[6]

Only six months had passed since Peter Sutcliffe's first attack; eleven more women were to die and five more were to survive horrific assaults before he was brought to justice. But the mythology that was to throw the investigation wildly off course had already had its monstrous birth; as a direct result, Sutcliffe would remain a free man for five more years. The police and the press had convinced themselves (and each other, the relationship between detectives and crime reporters being a symbiotic one) that they were dealing with a prostitute killer, a latter-day Jack the Ripper, that *this* was the significant link to look for in establishing which were the man's victims; from this point on, both evidence and suspects would be judged according to the yardstick of how well they measured up to the theory.

Three major errors flowed from the acceptance of this hypothesis. First, genuine Sutcliffe victims were excluded from the list of his crimes because they were the wrong 'type' of woman, while a murder in Preston which he did not commit *was* included on grounds of the unfortunate woman's character and habits. Second, the police fell into the trap of expecting the killer to behave like the nineteenth-century Ripper. Third, they convinced themselves that they 'knew' the killer in some mysterious and undefined way; that, if they were suddenly confronted with him, they would recognize him at once. George Oldfield, Assistant Chief Constable of West Yorkshire and sometime head of the Ripper Squad, said in 1980: 'If we had twenty or thirty suspects in one room we would know very quickly which one was the Ripper.'[7] Nor was this view confined to officers of the West Yorkshire Ripper Squad. A senior Manchester detective said much the same a couple of years before in 1978, affirming his belief that the killer had never been interviewed by the police

(Sutcliffe was first interviewed in 1977): 'When we do I am positive we will realize and nail him.'[8]

What did they expect? Someone slavering at the mouth who would throw back his cloak and flourish a blood-stained knife? Obviously not; what these confident statements were expressing was actually no more than a vague expectation of *difference*, that there would be something—a nervous gesture, a manner of speaking, staring eyes, a careless remark about prostitutes—that would single him out. Whoever he was, whatever his background, this man would be different from the rest, and from them: no wonder they were so seduced by the claim that he was a Geordie, an outsider, a foreigner in terms of long-established notions of Yorkshire and Lancashire rivalry, an idea they derived from a tape recording sent to them by a hoaxer purporting to be the killer. They were wrong, of course, not just about his coming from the north-east but also about the nature of his 'difference'. One of the chief ironies of the whole Yorkshire Ripper case is that the police spent millions of pounds fruitlessly searching for an outsider when the culprit was just an ordinary bloke, a local man who shared their background and attitudes to a remarkable degree. Sutcliffe was not a needle in a haystack: he was neither as conspicuous nor as alien as that image suggests. The task facing the police was more like sifting through bales of hay for a stray wisp of straw.

It is this feature, not Sutcliffe's difference but his *similarity* to other men, which becomes apparent as you get deeper into the case. In September 1979, increasingly desperate at their failure to catch the killer, West Yorkshire police compiled a summary of the information they had collected to date and the conclusions they had drawn from it. The dossier,[9] which runs to eighteen pages, was circulated to other police forces in Britain and around the world (the long gaps between some of the murders had led detectives to consider the theory that the killer worked or travelled abroad). It is a remarkable document, demonstrating how convinced the police were of the authenticity of the bogus taped message—suspects can be eliminated, it states confidently, if they do not have a 'North Eastern (Geordie) accent'. But its chief interest lies in the way it deals with the women believed to be Sutcliffe's victims, who are divided into two rigid groups, the 'prostitutes or women of loose morals' on whom the killer is said to have concentrated at the beginning of the series and the 'innocent' women who have become his prey towards the end. The 'innocent' victims include a building society clerk and a student, both of whom are considered by the police to have had valid reasons for being out alone at night (and both of whom, it might be added, clearly belong to one stratum or another of the middle classes). Into the other category is lumped just about everyone else, from women who worked as prostitutes to women who happened to go to the pub on their own in the evening to meet friends. It is clear that the division has been made on two grounds, one stated more explicitly than the other: first, that this is a case in which the early victims are morally flawed; and, second, that any woman who doesn't come from a middle-class family and who presumes to venture out alone at night is little better than a prostitute—a type of woman for whom, it is clear, the police themselves feel a barely concealed disgust. The first ground for the judgment rests on a highly suspect, circular piece of reasoning which goes as follows: the Yorkshire Ripper's early victims were tarts; Ms X was an early victim; Ms X is a tart; which *proves* that the Ripper's early victims were tarts. The second ground is bolstered with reference to individual women by the gratuitous inclusion of irrelevant and questionable information, such as the fact that one of them, a white woman, has had a black boyfriend. What the police failed to realize was that by including information of this sort they were actually approaching the case *backwards*, dredging up 'facts' of dubious standing (or, even worse, opinions dressed up as facts) in order to support a view they had already formed of the murderer's motive. Looked at logically, the killer could no more be aware that one victim had 'cohabited with several men', as the dossier meaningfully remarks, than he could know that another was a student at Bradford University. (The police line was, on the other hand, very useful to the defence at Sutcliffe's trial, since it appeared to support his claim that he was motivated by a hatred of prostitutes and only later turned to other women. He adhered to this line in spite of the fact that it was revealed at the trial that his first victim, Anna Rogulskyj, had rejected his approach in terms that made it clear she was not a prostitute: '. . . I asked her if she fancied it. She said, "Not on your life," and went to try and get into a house . . . I followed her and hit her with the hammer and she fell down.'[10]) The observations made in the police dossier about the earliest victims are simply ex post facto justifications of their own analysis of the case; as such, they tell the reader more about working-class male attitudes to what is and is not proper female conduct than about the mind of the killer. Here is what the document has to say about Mrs Rogulskyj, about whom Sutcliffe knew nothing other than that she had rejected his advance in no uncertain terms:

> She is a very heavy drinker and has cohabited with a
> number of men. She has a history of mental instability.

In July, 1975, she was associating with a local man who had moved into her home. She was apparently unhappy with her sexual relationship and left her home on the night of Friday, 4th July, 1975, saying she was going to Bradford to see her Jamaican boyfriend.

She visited Bradford that night and had some drink. About midnight she left 'Bibby's' Club and got a lift in a car with two Jamaicans who took her back to Keighley and dropped her off at home.

Whether these things are true or not, none of them could have been known to Peter Sutcliffe. To him, Mrs Rogulskyj was just a woman out alone at night, and one, moreover, who had made it plain she wanted nothing to do with him. The claims about her drinking, cohabiting with 'a number of men', and having a Jamaican boyfriend—and note that no evidence is produced for any of it—are there to show that Mrs Rogulskyj fits the police theory about the Ripper being a prostitute-hater; the implication, very clearly, is that she is a woman 'of loose morals'. The repeated reference to black men is perhaps one of the most interesting things about the character-sketch: since the dossier explicitly states that the murderer is not black (a suspect can be eliminated from the inquiry if he 'is an obvious coloured person'), its only purpose can be to tarnish further Mrs Rogulskyj's reputation—and in a way which is crudely racist.

Much the same process is applied to Mrs Smelt, the second victim to feature in the document:

Smelt is a married woman and lives with her husband. She is of loose morals.

It was her usual custom several nights a week to visit public houses in Halifax on her own.

Here we see the syllogism mentioned above in action, with a vengeance; there is no evidence for Mrs Smelt's alleged loose morals other than the fact that the police say it is so. (In a newspaper article published in 1983, after his retirement, the former Chief Constable of West Yorkshire, Ronald Gregory, went even further and casually dismissed Mrs Smelt as a 'prostitute'.[11]) Unless, that is, we accept the third sentence—the point of which surely is that Mrs Smelt, a married woman, went to public houses *without her husband*—as justification for the second, in which case it would be an extraordinary glimpse of police puritanism, had we not already seen on how flimsy a basis their judgments stand. Women who drink (we don't know how much), women who have boyfriends (especially if the women are white and the men are black), married women who go out without their husbands (even to meet *women* friends, which is what the dossier didn't explain in Mrs Smelt's case)—all are objects of disapprobation, not to say disgust. Women who worked as prostitutes fared even worse, with the police implying publicly that it was normal to hate them; in October 1979, a senior West Yorkshire detective, Jim Hobson, made this appeal to the Ripper at a press conference:

> He has made it clear that he hates prostitutes. Many people do. We, as a police force, will continue to arrest prostitutes. But the Ripper is now killing innocent girls. That indicates your mental state and that you are in urgent need of medical attention. You have made your point. Give yourself up before another innocent woman dies.[12]

Even Sutcliffe, at his trial, did not go quite this far: he did at least claim that he was demented all the time and had a divine 'mission' to kill prostitutes. But the thrust of Hobson's widely reported remarks is clear—the Ripper's madness manifested itself only when he turned to 'innocent girls'. At another press conference on the Ripper murders, in Manchester in 1979, when I was working for a local radio station, I received a crude but less chilling insight into the police view of prostitutes. Filing into a room where, earlier the same day, the Manchester Ripper Squad had been playing the bogus Geordie tape to local prostitutes, a male reporter called to the most senior policeman present, Jack Ridgway: 'Here, Jack, I hope we won't catch anything from sitting on these chairs?' Ridgway replied: 'I don't know, I kept out of their way just in case.' (Moments before this exchange took place, Ridgway called out to me, one of only two female journalists present, 'Sorry, love, you're too late, the pros' conference is over,' apparently blind to the notebook and heavy tape-recorder I was carrying. A prostitute, it seems, is any woman in the wrong place at the wrong time.) Even when Sutcliffe had been caught, and the full extent of his crimes was clear, some policemen persisted in speaking of the prostitute victims with as much distaste as they did the killer. A senior West Yorkshire detective, discussing eighteen-year-old Elena Rytka with one of my colleagues from the *Sunday Times* (where I was then working), gleefully announced: 'Her fanny was as sticky as a paper-hanger's bucket.' It seemed to me that a gloating disgust was a curious emotion to feel on contemplation of the mutilated body of a dead teenage girl.

How on earth, given their own attitudes to women and female sexuality, did the police expect to be able to recognize the killer if they came face to face with him? If, as they believed, the man was disgusted by prostitutes—well, so were they. If he expressed disapproval of married women going to pubs without their husbands, or said he couldn't stand women who drank too much, or remarked that women who went out alone late at night were no better than whores, would they really think something was wrong about this one and arrest him? Or would they dismiss him as an average bloke, the kind who can be found leaning on the bar in the local pub—not to mention the police club—any night of the week?

If they hadn't a chance of spotting the Ripper through his aberrant behaviour, the police were going to have to rely on good old-fashioned police work—clues. Unfortunately, here too they were undermined by their insistence that the criminal was a prostitute killer. The police dossier on the murders, having dealt with Mrs Rogulskyj and Mrs Smelt, is then notable for an omission. It moves straight on to October 1975 and Wilma McCann, the Scottish woman who, they believed, occasionally worked as a prostitute, leaving out all mention of Tracey Browne, the schoolgirl attacked near Keighley in August that year. The non-appearance of Miss Browne was explained in an article which appeared in the *Sunday Times* in November 1981, six months after Sutcliffe's trial. It said:

Detectives failed to uncover an almost perfect photofit likeness and description of Sutcliffe dating back to August, 1975, soon after his attacks began. A 14-year-old schoolgirl, Tracey Browne, survived the head injuries she received in an unsolved attack which bore all the hallmarks of what later was clearly identified as Ripper attacks. Yet, amazingly, she was never included as a Ripper victim, despite the fact that the first official Ripper attack, a serious assault on Anna Rogulski [sic], took place in Keighley only a few weeks earlier.[13]

The omission is not as extraordinary as it seems. The Ripper dossier states quite categorically that 'most of the earlier victims are prostitutes or women of loose moral character'. That this should be so is *essential* to the police concept of the attacks as the work of a latterday Jack the Ripper. Mrs Rogulskyj and Mrs Smelt, both adult women, can—with a little massaging of the facts—just about be made to fit the pattern. A fourteen-year-old schoolgirl who was attacked in a small, pretty Yorkshire town is another matter. Out goes Miss Browne—if she was ever even considered as a potential Sutcliffe victim—and with her goes 'an almost perfect photofit likeness' of Sutcliffe.

The process does, however, work both ways. If Miss Browne can be excluded on the grounds that she is the 'wrong' type of woman, another woman can be added to the list because she does match the police concept of the standard Ripper victim. The victim who appears in the police dossier after Wilma McCann is the pitiful Joan Mary Harrison, brutally murdered in a disused garage in November 1975. The important thing to bear in mind about Mrs Harrison is that, unlike Miss Browne, she was unquestionably *not* a Ripper victim—Sutcliffe always categorically denied responsibility for this killing, and he was not charged with it—and there was every reason why detectives should have approached the decision to include her on the list with extreme circumspection. Her death took place in Preston, Lancashire, miles away from the Leeds-Bradford conurbation where the vast majority of the crimes were committed—a good distance even from Manchester, where two genuine Ripper murders did take place. The killing bore little resemblance to those in the Ripper series. Although Mrs Harrison's clothing had been disarranged, the murderer did not use a hammer, knife or screwdriver, the characteristic Ripper weapons; there was a wound to the back of her head which appeared to have been made with a shoe heel, and

Mrs Harrison had been kicked to death in an attack that caused extensive injuries not just to the top of her head and the trunk but also to the face and legs. (When the police came to add Mrs Harrison to the toll of Ripper victims in 1978, they got round part of this problem by deciding the original post-mortem finding was wrong, and that the head injury was 'consistent with being struck by a hammer-type instrument'.) A further warning sign was the fact that Mrs Harrison had a bite mark on one of her breasts, an injury quite unlike that of any other victim. In a complete break with the Ripper pattern, her handbag and purse had been stolen. Above all, there had been a considerable degree of sexual activity prior to the woman's death: the killer had had sexual intercourse with Mrs Harrison *and* buggered her.

It is this last feature of the Harrison case which is most striking; long before Sutcliffe was caught it was clear that the purpose of his attacks was not direct sexual gratification in the form of intercourse but the mutilations carried out after the women had been rendered helpless by blows to the head. On the contrary, the murderer went out of his way to *avoid* direct sexual contact with the women he attacked; the semen on Wilma McCann's trousers was the result of his masturbating over her body. Why, in this one case, should he have changed the pattern and carried out a *double* sexual assault on the victim? The police could, of course, point to one other atypical case which they believed to be the work of the Ripper: that of Yvonne Pearson, a young woman who had convictions for working as a prostitute and who was murdered in Bradford in January 1978. Miss Pearson—who, the official dossier pointedly informs us, lived with 'a West Indian'—had massive head injuries, probably caused by a boulder, and had been jumped on in the chest area. But this murder did at least take place in a city, Bradford, in which other obvious Ripper victims had been attacked; additionally, Miss

Pearson was not robbed, nor did any sexual interference take place, and the killer concentrated his attack on a part of the body consistent with other Ripper murders. (Sutcliffe later explained that this was an opportunistic, unplanned attack, and he did not have his usual weapons at hand.) The killing, then, though not precisely fitting the established Ripper pattern, did not deviate from it as obviously as the attack on Mrs Harrison in Preston. I say this not merely with the advantage of hindsight; in November 1980, a matter of days after the murder of Jacqueline Hill in Leeds and six weeks *before* Sutcliffe was arrested, the *Sunday Times* Insight team, of which I was then a member, published an analysis of the police dossier on the murders. It concluded that the discrepancies between the Preston murder and the other Ripper attacks were so great as to cast doubt on the decision to include it on the list of Ripper crimes. Having studied the pattern of the killer, it said, 'there is no easy way to account for the fate of Joan Harrison'.[14] The article discounted the suggestion, advanced by a psychiatrist, that the Preston case was a 'trial run' after which the Ripper, having established that sexual activity did not afford him satisfaction, turned his attention to mutilation; it also raised the possibility that the police were relying on forensic evidence from the Preston murder when it was not part of the series. This is exactly what was happening even though, in the same article, George Oldfield, the assistant chief constable of West Yorkshire, admitted publicly that the case of Mrs Harrison was 'the most dubious of all'.

Why, then, was Mrs Harrison included on the official list of Ripper victims? The answer is simple: because, unlike Tracey Browne, she matched almost exactly the police notion of the classic Ripper victim. Detectives were working from a sort of mental photofit of the victim as much as from a real photofit of the killer, and Mrs Harrison could not have been a better match, as the Ripper dossier makes clear:

> Harrison had cohabited with various men in the Leyland, Chorley and Preston areas and since June, 1975, she had been living with a man in Preston.
>
> She was a chronic alcoholic and had close associations with other alcoholics, drug addicts and prostitutes in the Preston area. She had previous convictions for theft and, although not convicted of prostitution, it is known she resorted to this in order to provide money for her drinking habits.

Sixteen months after her murder, in March 1977, a senior West Yorkshire detective told the *Yorkshire Post*:

> We are also following up a possible link with a similar type of murder in Preston in November 1975, when a prostitute was found stabbed to death in the town centre.[15]

The slip about the cause of death is revealing; Mrs Harrison is 'a prostitute', the Ripper's preferred type of victim, and therefore the manner in which she died hardly matters. When, a year later in March 1978, a letter posted in Sunderland arrived at police headquarters in Leeds claiming responsibility for the Preston killing as well as the other murders, the inquiry began to head inexorably for disaster. The author of the letter not only signed himself 'Jack the Ripper', he even behaved like him; one of the things people 'know' about the Whitechapel killer is that he loved to taunt the police and did so in letters to them. The

Sunderland correspondent addressed the first of his letters to
George Oldfield and mocked the police for their inability to
catch him. It was an illiterate effort and said, in part:

> You and your mates havent a clue. That photo in the
> paper gave me fits. And that lot about killing myself, no
> chance. I have got things to do. My purpose to rid the
> streets of them sluts . . . Up to number eight now you
> say seven but remember Preston 75. Get about, you know
> you were right I travel a bit.[16]

It contained a postscript, promising 'Old slut next time I
hope'. There was every reason to treat the letter, and one posted
five days later to the *Daily Mirror* in Manchester, with extreme
caution. For a start, the inquiry had been plagued by anonymous
letters in the same way as had the investigation into the crimes
of Jack the Ripper a century before; hundreds of letters poured
into police stations and newspaper offices up and down the country from people claiming to be the Yorkshire Ripper (I remember one such communication arriving at the *Sunday Times* which
consisted of a postcard picture of the chapel at Leeds University
adorned with a swastika, and claimed to give details of where the
body of the next victim could be found. The police were called
and ruled it out as a hoax.) If the letter to Oldfield sounded
genuine, it was because its author had taken care to mimic the
first letter to bear the signature 'Jack the Ripper' in the nineteenth-century police inquiry, a missive sent to the Central News
Agency in September 1888 and which began:

> I keep on hearing the police have caught me but they
> won't fix me just yet. I have laughed when they look so

clever and talk about being on the right track. That joke about Leather Apron [the suggestion that this was what the killer wore] gave me real fits. I am down on whores and I shan't quit ripping them till I do get buckled.[17]

The parallels are obvious: the taunts directed at the police, the repetition of the unusual phrase 'gave me [real] fits', the assertion that the killer's motive is hatred of prostitutes. They do little more than suggest that the person who wrote to Oldfield had read one of the many books about the Whitechapel killer, most of which quote the various 'Ripper' letters. Most of these, including the one quoted above, are of doubtful authenticity, as Donald Rumbelow explains in his book *The Complete Jack the Ripper*.[18] But West Yorkshire police were hoist with their own petard; they had expected their killer to act like Jack the Ripper, or their *idea* of how that criminal behaved, and here was someone who was doing just that. In addition, the letter to Oldfield, and the one which followed it a few days later, seems to have appealed to the detective's vanity; it confirmed a belief he maintained throughout the Yorkshire Ripper investigation, namely, the conviction that the twentieth-century killer had a personal interest in him. The second letter, written in the same hand, posted in Sunderland, and addressed to the *Daily Mirror* in Manchester, began:

I have already written chief constable George Oldfield a man 'I respect' Concerning the recent Ripper murders I told him and I am telling you to warn them whores I'll strike again and soon when heat cools off . . . Up to number eight now You say seven but remember Preston 75.[19]

Oldfield believed that the Yorkshire Ripper was addressing him directly just as Jack the Ripper had addressed George Lusk, head of the Whitechapel Vigilance Committee, in the single letter from the Victorian case with some claim to authenticity (although not signed 'Jack the Ripper', it was accompanied by a piece of human kidney which appeared to have been cut from the body of one of the victims, Catherine Eddowes). A year later, after receiving another letter and then a cassette tape from the same correspondent, Oldfield said: 'I would like to talk to this man. And I feel he wants to talk to me. This has become something of a feud. He obviously wants to outwit me, but I won't pack it in until he's caught'.[20]

Nevertheless, there was still a compelling reason to doubt the authenticity of the Sunderland letters. The first and second in the sequence boasted that the writer had killed eight women rather than seven, referring to Joan Harrison—'Preston 75'—as the extra victim. But only two weeks after the first letter arrived, the body of another Ripper victim, Yvonne Pearson, was discovered in Bradford. She had been missing since January, and had certainly been dead for some time when the letters were written. If the correspondence was genuine, and the killer was eager to show off about the number of his victims, why did he fail to mention the latest Bradford killing? The obvious inference was that he did not know about it, and that he was not the Yorkshire Ripper. This was not what the police wanted to believe. The writer had conformed to the behaviour pattern they expected, down to viewing the case, like them, as a species of TV-drama police versus outlaw. They pointed out that the postscript to the first letter had promised that the next victim would be 'old'; the next woman to die, Vera Millward in Manchester, was forty-one—far from elderly, but certainly considerably older than those who immediately preceded her, eighteen-year-old Elena Rytka and twenty-two-year-old Yvonne Pearson. When the third letter arrived a year later in March 1979, they reasoned that it contained two further proofs of authenticity. One of them was a reference to Mrs Millward's medical history. The letter remarked on the coincidence that she had, some time before her death, been treated in Manchester Royal Infirmary, the hospital in whose grounds her body was found—information that, according to the police, had never been made public and must have been passed on by Mrs Millward to her killer. In this assumption they were simply wrong, as the Chief Constable, Ronald Gregory, admitted after Sutcliffe's trial; the detail had previously been mentioned in an article in the *Daily Mail*. In his account of the murder hunt published in the *Mail on Sunday* in 1983, Gregory revealed that a detective chief inspector from Northumbria police—the force in whose area the Geordie sender of the letters and tapes was supposed to live—had in autumn 1979 'studied every newspaper article written about our inquiry and proved that everything in the letters could have been gleaned from them'. Gregory went on:

> He also compared the phraseology and vocabulary used by the 1888 Ripper and again found striking similarities. His conclusion was that the Geordie was obviously immersed in the Ripper myth and like the original Victorian criminal craved publicity. So it could be an elaborate hoax.[21]

The Northumbria policeman was right, although even he seems to have absorbed an element of the myth surrounding the Victorian Ripper—the belief that the murderer longed for publicity. West Yorkshire police, who embraced the myth wholeheartedly, were wrong. This did not prevent them from releasing snippets from the letters to the press as if they were the genuine article; they had an emotional conviction that they knew their man, and the tone of the letters was in keeping with their image of him.

They also had their other 'proof', the fact that the man who licked the third envelope was a B-sector, someone whose blood group is the rare group B, and who secretes traces of it into his bodily fluids, primarily semen and saliva. In this he was identical to the murderer of Joan Harrison, whose blood group was known to the police through his semen; this point, along with the references in the letters to 'Preston 75', appeared conclusive to them. That is why, when a cassette tape from the same man arrived three months after the third letter, they decided to allow the public to hear the flat, Geordie voice taunting George Old-field with his failure to catch the Ripper: 'I reckon your boys are letting you down, George, ya can't be much good, can ya?'[22]

Their logic was false; moreover, they had fallen into a trap of their own making. There were at least two other and more plausible explanations of the letters and tape: first, that they were the work of someone who had followed the case closely in the press and, by an unfortunate coincidence, had the same blood group as the man who killed Joan Harrison; second, that the letters and tape had been sent by her murderer, *who was not the Yorkshire Ripper*. The truth may never be known, but the process by which the entire country was misled into looking for a Geordie killer is clear. West Yorkshire police decided, against the evidence, that they were looking for a prostitute killer, a modern-day Jack the Ripper, and that Joan Harrison, who occasionally worked as a prostitute, could be one of his victims. They care-lessly let this opinion be known in the press. When letters began to arrive which mentioned the Preston murder, they decided the reference was highly significant, even though the writer inexplicably failed to claim responsibility for another of the Ripper murders; they felt the tenor of the letters fitted the Jack the Ripper pattern. When the third letter arrived, they decided that saliva tests linked it to the Preston killing and a reference to Mrs Millward to the Ripper murders. Because the tape which arrived next was in an envelope addressed in the same handwriting, they concluded that it, too, was genuine. The Yorkshire Ripper was now officially a Geordie.

In the summer of 1979, when two detective constables interviewed Peter Sutcliffe—the fifth time he had been seen by police in the course of the inquiry—one of them was struck by Sutcliffe's resemblance to the photofit provided by one of the survivors, Marilyn Moore. He also noticed that Sutcliffe had a gap between his front teeth, as the killer was thought to have, and had the right foot size for boot prints found at the scene of the murders. A check with criminal records even produced a minor criminal record, for going equipped to steal. The detective was sufficiently suspicious to recommend that Sutcliffe should be further investigated. Because he was not a Geordie, and his handwriting did not match that in the letters, the report was simply filed. Three more women were to die, two more survive murderous attacks before the new 'Jack the Ripper' made a foolish mistake and gave himself way.

Sutcliffe's trial opened on 29 April 1981, a Wednesday. He was charged with the murder of thirteen women: Wilma McCann, Emily Jackson, Irene Richardson, Patricia Atkinson, Jayne MacDonald, Jean Jordan, Yvonne Pearson, Elena Rytka, Vera Millward, Josephine Whitaker, Barbara Leach, Marguerite Walls and Jacqueline Hill. He also faced seven counts of attempted murder involving Anna Rogulskyj, Olive Smelt, Marcella Claxton,

Maureen Long, Marilyn Moore, Upadhya Bandara and Teresa Sykes. An agreement had been reached before the trial started; the prosecution, represented by the Attorney-General, Sir Michael Havers, was ready to accept Sutcliffe's plea of not guilty to murder but guilty of manslaughter on grounds of diminished responsibility. To the surprise of both defence and prosecution the judge, Mr Justice Boreham, refused to go along with this deal and insisted that the trial go ahead. Just over three weeks later, on Friday 22 May, Sutcliffe was found guilty as charged by a majority verdict of ten to two. He was sent to prison for life.

The issue which had faced the jury was this: was Sutcliffe a clever criminal, aware of what he was doing and determined to avoid capture, or was he mad? The four psychiatrists who gave evidence at the trial were agreed on the latter view, attaching to Sutcliffe's condition the label paranoid schizophrenia. In interviews before the trial he had told them about voices from God and a 'mission' to kill prostitutes—classic symptoms of paranoid schizophrenia. The jury's decision was a rejection of this view, influenced no doubt by the evidence of a prison officer who overheard a conversation between Sutcliffe and his wife Sonia in which the accused man said: 'I am going to do a long time in prison, thirty years or more, unless I can convince people in here I am mad and maybe then ten years in the loony bin.'[23] When the trial was over, Sutcliffe began serving his sentence in prison. Since then, in a development which the psychiatrists see as vindicating their stance at the Old Bailey, he has been diagnosed as mad and moved to a top-security hospital, Broadmoor. Are they right?

In a sense, it is the wrong question. The battle that was fought out in court—the mad/bad dichotomy—both substitutes for and obscures the real dilemma raised by the Yorkshire Ripper case: is Sutcliffe a one-off, *sui generis* as I have heard one psychiatrist describe him, someone who stands outside our culture and has no relation to it? Those who assert that Sutcliffe is mad are in essence saying yes to this question; madness is a closed category, one over which we have no control and for which we bear no responsibility. The deranged stand apart from us; we cannot be *blamed* for their insanity. Thus the urge to characterize Sutcliffe as mad has powerful emotional origins; it has as much to do with how we see ourselves and the society in which we live as it has to do with our perception of him and of his crimes. It is a *distancing* mechanism, a way of establishing a comforting gulf between ourselves and a particularly unacceptable criminal. This accounts for the difficulty in pinning down what people mean when they describe Sutcliffe as mad. Throughout the period in which they were vainly searching for the killer, West Yorkshire police regularly described him in this way (George Oldfield called him 'a nutter'[24]). So did newspaper articles and the general public. But there is a great deal of confusion here, as became plain whenever someone tried to explain in what way Sutcliffe was mad. Clearly it is not the act of killing per se which characterizes someone as deranged. Most convicted murderers end up in prison, not in secure hospitals. (We do not even regard all killing as bad; although we live in a society which, especially since the abolition of the death penalty for murder, cherishes something called the right to life, most of us implicitly accept that there are all sorts of circumstances in which that right is overruled by others. The most obvious example is war, when the right to life is temporarily put aside in defence of concepts like freedom and self-determination. But there are others: abortion law in Britain permits the destruction of unborn life in limited circumstances; since 1980, there has effectively been an extra-judicial death penalty for terrorists operating within the jurisdiction of British forces. The lack of public outcry in cases like the Iranian embassy

siege of that year, when terrorists were shot dead by the SAS
*after* they had surrendered, suggests that this unacknowledged
policy has met with a considerable degree of public approval.)
If it is not the fact that Sutcliffe is a murderer which makes him
mad, what else is it? Is it the sheer *number* of his crimes? But there
are double murderers, even triple murderers, who are tried and
sent to prison rather than to a secure hospital. Is it the *nature* of
the killings? Sane people have committed atrocities, as evidenced
in the Nazi concentration camps. So is it his motive, the crusade
against prostitutes which was claimed on his behalf and which
Sutcliffe himself used as his defence when he was caught? Even
this is not universally regarded as the *locus* of his madness. For
Jim Hobson, Acting Assistant Chief Constable of West Yorkshire, in remarks already quoted, the killer's crusade against prostitutes was understandable; his madness manifested itself only
when he turned to 'innocent girls'. The *Yorkshire Evening Post*,
in a message to the killer printed after the murder of Jayne
MacDonald, was merely confused:

> You have killed five times now . . . Your motive, it is
> believed, is a dreadful hatred of prostitutes, a hate that
> drives you to slash and bludgeon your victims. But,
> inevitably, that twisted passion went horribly wrong on
> Sunday night. An innocent sixteen-year-old lass, a
> happy, respectable working-class girl from a decent
> Leeds family, crossed your path. How did you feel yes-
> terday when you learned that your bloodstained cru-
> sade had gone so horribly wrong? . . . Sick in mind
> though you undoubtedly are, there must have been
> some remorse as you rid yourself of Jayne's blood-
> stains.[25]

There seems to be an implication here that, while the killer has always been mad, he is somehow madder now that an 'innocent sixteen-year-old lass' has become his prey. It is hard to believe that the author of the letter really meant what he or she appears to be saying: that someone has to be a little bit mad to kill prostitutes, but is completely deranged only if he slaughters ordinary women.

The psychiatrists who appeared at Sutcliffe's trial did little better. They had no choice but to arrive at a conclusion about his mental state, since their testimony as expert witnesses was crucial to his defence, but their diagnosis appeared to be based largely on what Sutcliffe said, rather than on what he had actually done. (One of them, Dr Malcolm MacCulloch, medical director of Park Lane Special Hospital in Liverpool, told the court it had taken him only thirty minutes to decide that Sutcliffe was a paranoid schizophrenic.[26]) In approaching the case like this the doctors were just as confused as everyone else. If Sutcliffe was mad, as they came to believe, was he really a reliable witness on the question of his own motivation? But if he was sane, wasn't it possible that he was lying when he claimed to have heard voices from God telling him to wipe out prostitutes? The doctors accepted Sutcliffe's story of a 'mission' as evidence of his paranoid schizophrenia, a type of madness in which the subject suffers delusions. This was their, and his, downfall. The prosecution pointed out that Sutcliffe, who was supposed to be mad, had nevertheless had the sense to conceal these voices from even the closest members of his family, including his wife and his adored mother, who was still alive when he first heard them; that he had taken immense pains not to be caught, even changing his method of attack to strangulation in the penultimate murder to throw police off the scent; that he had made several remarks about feigning madness while on remand; and that his wife had been treated for paranoid schizophrenia years before—her delusions were even, like his, of a religious nature, taking the form of a belief that she was Jesus—giving him plenty of opportunity to observe and later mimic her symptoms. It is hardly surprising, in the circumstances, that the jury rejected Sutcliffe's defence and sent him to prison.

The point of all this is simply to demonstrate the futility of trying to make sense of Sutcliffe's acts with the rigid mad/bad dichotomy as a starting-point. Yet, if we cannot allot to Sutcliffe's claims the status of unimpeachable testimony, how are we to answer any other question about the case, such as the one I raised earlier in place of the mad/bad dilemma: namely, whether the Yorkshire Ripper case stands in a class of its own with no meaning for us, or whether it has anything to say about the nature of our society?

There is a way to approach this inquiry, and it is so obvious that it is all the more perplexing that it should have been more or less ignored in favour of asking the murderer to make his own diagnosis. It is to look in some detail at what Sutcliffe actually *did* rather than what he later said about it. Such an inquiry is distasteful, involving the repetition of a catalogue of mutilations, but I believe it is justified by our failure, up until now, to grasp the significance of the Yorkshire Ripper murders. (An honourable exception to this rule is the poet Blake Morrison, whose 'Ballad of the Yorkshire Ripper' reveals a precise understanding of the meaning of the case.)

The pattern of the attacks has already been outlined: one or more blows to the head to incapacitate the victim, followed by mutilation of the trunk—occasionally the wounds were to the back, more often to the front. In almost every case, the victim's clothes were moved—her bra pulled up over her breasts, her pants pulled down. Sutcliffe never stabbed through clothing. The mutilations were carried out on specific areas of the exposed torso with a variety of weapons ranging from a hacksaw blade to a knife to a sharpened Phillips screwdriver. The attacks were frenzied, and often involved multiple stab wounds through the same opening. They were concentrated on the chest and breasts, the abdomen and the vagina. One victim was stabbed twenty-five times in the abdomen, breasts, thighs and vagina. The screwdriver used in this attack was also used on another victim, a woman who was stabbed in the abdomen and shoulder blade eight times. In another case, Sutcliffe returned to the body eight days later and inflicted an additional eighteen stab wounds on her breasts, chest, stomach and vagina. Some of the wounds were eight inches deep. In several of the murders, he removed the victim's shoes or boots and placed them on top of her body; one woman had a boot print on her thigh.

Many people have asked how, having carried out one of these horrific attacks, Sutcliffe could return home and behave normally. They are looking at the case back to front. Far from the murders making him unable to live with himself, *Sutcliffe was able to live with himself only because of them*. The common denominator in the attacks is Sutcliffe's obsessional destruction of those parts of the female body which signal gender. It was not enough for him to know from her general appearance that his victim was a woman; he had to see the proof with his own eyes in the shape of her breasts, her waist, her hips, her pubic hair. A single blow was not enough; he had to strike repeatedly to gain relief. Sometimes he left one of his victim's shoes or boots on her body as a symbol of his power, evidence of the way in which he had trampled his victim underfoot. These are the actions of a man to whom femininity was a threat, who hated and feared it so much that his survival depended on his capacity to locate and annihilate it. He carried out these search-and-destroy missions again and

again, using any woman who came within his reach, whether she
happened to be a schoolgirl, a tired and pain-racked prostitute,
or a medical student from Singapore; the urge was so strong that
any woman would do, regardless of her age or class or occupation. (When his early attacks on non-prostitute women failed,
leaving them horribly injured but alive, he turned to more easily
available victims—prostitutes—changing his *modus operandi* once
again when the red-light districts became too hot.) In destroying
women's bodies, he challenged and conquered the terrible thing
he could never acknowledge: the feminine part of himself.

The striking thing that emerged about Sutcliffe after his trial,
when a flood of reminiscence from family and friends provided
pages of copy in newspapers, magazines and books, was the
fragility of his masculine identity. He was born and brought up
in the small Yorkshire town of Bingley, a few miles south of the
Haworth parsonage where, a century before, the Brontë sisters
had written novels vividly expressing their intuitive grasp of the
fatal consequences of masculinity. To this day, Bingley is a
community with rigid notions about the behaviour appropriate
to each sex, and Sutcliffe always had an uneasy relationship with
the mode of conduct he knew to be appropriate to him. When
he grew up and became a lorry driver, he placed in the cab a
handwritten notice which stated: 'In this truck is a man whose
latent genius if unleashed would rock the nation, whose dynamic
energy would overpower those around him. Better let him
sleep?'[27] It was a piece of wishful thinking on Sutcliffe's part; his
boss at the lorry firm, William Clark, said later: 'He was a very
good worker but he had a strange mental make-up. Criticism
would make his eyes fill with tears.'[28]

Peter Sutcliffe had always been, in the eyes of the brawling,
macho family in which he grew up, a bit of a sissy—sensitive,

not keen on games, a mummy's boy. His mother Kathleen Sutcliffe, née Coonan, was a devout Roman Catholic and bore six
children, one of whom died in infancy. Peter, born in 1946, was
the eldest. In his book about the family, '. . . *Somebody's Husband,
Somebody's Son*', Gordon Burn describes the young Peter as a
child who never wanted to go out and play, something which
his father, John Sutcliffe, found 'very peculiar'. Burn writes:

> By the age of five Peter still hadn't got out of the habit
> of clinging limpet-like to his mother's hems. And even
> when he was seven his father would look out of the
> window and see him and his mother and, usually, another
> woman coming up the road from school: the other
> woman's children would be walking by her side, casually
> holding her hands; Peter though would be largely invisi-
> ble in the camouflage of his mother's skirts.[29]

Peter was educated at Catholic schools and, though bright,
left school at fifteen. He, like the other children, went in fear of
John Sutcliffe, as one of them, Peter's youngest brother Carl,
described to Gordon Burn:

> We were all frightened to death of me dad. He were like
> a monster. He were never in house, but when he was he
> ruled the roost. When he came in drunk we'd all sit there
> in fear; you didn't move. Whatever was on television, no
> matter how many were watching, was straight off and
> switched over to what he wanted to see, which were
> usually sport. If cricket come on, that were it. He used
> to sort of edge up to telly and sit right in front of it.
> Nobody dare say owt.

Oh Christ, he had a foul temper. I seen Maureen [his
sister] get a beating off him when she was about fifteen,
an' he once beat me black and blue when I were a kid.[30]

John Sutcliffe was also violent to his wife, and a far from
faithful husband. At one time he courted a crippled single woman
who was simultaneously the object of his own father's attentions.
His father, Arthur, was known locally as a 'ladies' man'; barely
on speaking terms with his wife, John's mother and Peter's grand-
mother, he carried on affairs with other women in a caravan
dubbed the 'passion wagon'. John was proud of being a chip off
the old block; he would boast to his teenage sons that he'd been
with a 'right cracker' the previous night. On the one occasion
when Kathleen tried to turn the tables, her husband discovered
that she had a man friend and impersonated him on the phone,
luring her to a meeting at a hotel where he triumphantly confronted her. A couple of years later, John Sutcliffe left Kathleen
to live with a neighbour, a deaf and dumb woman—a particularly suitable choice, it might be thought, for a man with his
entirely functional view of women. He returned to his wife, he
told Gordon Burn, only when 'it was obvious to me she'd been
taught her lesson'.[31]

Peter, the most sensitive of Kathleen's children, seems to have
vacillated between rejecting the life-style of his father and some
of his brothers—Mick, in particular, seems to have been more
than happy to follow in John's footsteps—and trying to keep up
with it. In an interview with the *Evening Standard* published after
Peter's arrest, Mick said:

The police have had me in several times for the Ripper
murders because I've got form for grievous bodily harm,
actual bodily harm and a bit of burglary. But I didn't

know they suspected Peter. I can't imagine that he is guilty. He used to be a right one for fighting when he was younger but now he's quite happy to have a drink once a week and go to the pictures.[32]

Peter's adult life was, in fact, a mass of contradictions. He was often quiet and reserved, but the exhibitionist side of his nature emerged at work, especially when he was employed as a grave-digger at Bingley cemetery in 1964 at the age of eighteen. There he displayed a macabre sense of humour, boasting about the jewellery he said he had stolen from rotting corpses when open-ing up graves for new burials. He also earned a bit of money on the side, washing cadavers for firms of undertakers. He had few girlfriends, giving the impression of being uninterested in women, but nevertheless was keen to compete with his brother Mick's knowledge of the local red-light districts. Mick told Burn:

He used to tek us round red light districts in motor an' say, 'This is the best spot to get 'em.' He thought he were showing me summat new, but I knew already. He'd say, 'Look at these here.' So I'd fuckin' look at them, and that's all I'd want to do. 'Look at this old scraggly cunt,' he'd say, 'coming towards us.' Then he'd wind window down and ask how much. 'A fiver,' she'd say. 'Oh fuck off,' he'd shout, and we'd just drive off.[33]

Burn adds: 'This behaviour bore no resemblance to the thoughtful, gentle, courteous Peter whom everybody knew at home, the Peter who was always especially conspicuous at Christ-mas.'

It was the quiet, well-mannered side of Peter's character which appealed to his wife Sonia, who was a shy and unworldly girl of sixteen when he met her in 1967 (Peter was then twenty-one). Sonia Szurma's family was a cut above Peter's; unlike his sisters, Sonia wanted a career as a teacher. Her parents had come to Britain from Czechoslovakia and were interested in the books and music which had no place in the Sutcliffe household. Sonia was nervous and withdrawn but she was Peter's passport to a new life. She also appealed to the protective attitude to women which had developed in him during the years he spent watching his father ignore and mistreat his mother; particularly after her breakdown in 1972, two years before they married, Sonia needed a great deal of looking after.

As he courted Sonia Peter was, in effect, leading a double life. The couple would go out with Peter's sister Maureen and her boyfriend, a soldier in the Royal Engineers called Robin Holland. Holland later remembered:

> The four of us, Sonia, Maureen, Peter and me, used to go out regularly together for a drink. The Sutcliffe family often used to have parties for one thing or another and Peter always had plenty to say for himself. The favourite conversation, more a sermon really, was men who two-timed their wives. He used to call them 'beasts'. In fact the rest of the family seemed to think Peter was a saint, sort of the perfect son. But I know he wasn't. I had regularly gone out with him drinking to pubs in the red light districts and his main topic of conversation had been sex and prostitutes.[34]

Peter's marriage in 1974 was soon followed by the purchase of a house in Heaton, a middle-class suburb of Bradford. The move meant that the boy from the noisy, crowded council house had progressed into a world where masculine bravado was no longer at a premium. But his confusion, and the pressure on him to conform to the notions with which he had grown up, was internal. While he appeared to Sonia to be a kind, considerate husband, while he took pains to compensate for his previously poor work record by gaining his HGV licence and becoming a valued employee of a haulage company, he was still going out with friends to tour pubs and red-light districts. He would frequently disparage prostitutes, and boast about occasions when he had cheated them out of payment. Peter's father, John, predictably failed to grasp this point, claiming in the *Sunday Mirror* after the trial that Sonia was the cause of his son's crimes:

> I am convinced things could have worked out differently had Peter married a girl more on his own level who didn't have so many problems of her own. Peter exchanged a loving, warm and caring family background for a claustrophobic and rigid existence in Sonia's world.[35]

The atmosphere in Garden Lane, Heaton, was certainly different from that in the Sutcliffe household. To John, it was simply unthinkable that his eldest son could prefer the quiet existence he shared with Sonia, who had now qualified as a teacher, to the rough-and-tumble he had grown up with in Bingley. His analysis, that Peter's criminal career was somehow Sonia's fault, was shared by the *Daily Mirror*, which wrote:

> He worshipped her. She dominated him. Both hid their thoughts behind a mask of reserve.
> There were tantrums and tears. But never in public. Only behind the respectable façade of their Bradford home did the mask drop. Then Sonia, shy and frail to the

world outside, would often become the nagging wife. And in Sutcliffe, pent-up fury would build to a destructive force.

He did not lift a finger against his wife.

One senior Ripper squad detective said: 'I think when Sutcliffe attacked his twenty victims, he was attacking his wife twenty times in his mind.'[36]

Such speculation is, once again, approaching the case backwards. Peter's marriage was not the *cause* of his violence but an attempt to contain it. He inhabited a world in which violence to women—wives, girlfriends, prostitutes—was a routine part of life. One of his closest friends was Trevor Birdsall, a man with whom he frequently visited red-light districts to shout abuse at prostitutes. One evening in 1969, the two men were out together in Bradford. Peter got out of the car, returning a few minutes later to say that he'd attacked 'one of the bags' with a brick wrapped in a sock. The brick had fallen out; he showed Birdsall the empty sock.[37] Six years later, in 1975, the two men went drinking together in Halifax. On the way home, passing a quiet residential district, Peter spotted a woman he'd noticed earlier in a pub. Her name, which he did not know, was Olive Smelt. He again stopped the car, disappeared for a few minutes, and was unusually quiet during the rest of the journey. When he read about the attack on Mrs Smelt in the local paper, Birdsall's suspicions were aroused. But he did nothing. It took him five years to send an anonymous letter about Peter to the police, a letter which he followed up with an unproductive visit to them a few days later, only a matter of weeks before Peter was caught.

Birdsall's behaviour, which caused much comment at the time of Sutcliffe's trial, is not difficult to understand. Though he was regarded, like Peter, as something of a sissy by some of the people who knew him, he was thoroughly imbued with the same brutal working-class culture which shaped the lives of Peter's father and his brother Mick. Birdsall's wife, Melissa, had lost a leg in a car crash as a child, but this did not stop her husband beating her up on a regular basis.[38] If Sutcliffe *had* knocked about a couple of women—and Birdsall hadn't actually seen him do it—it wasn't as if Peter had done something which he hadn't done himself. Peter's sport lay outside the family, that was all, while Birdsall got his fun at home. Peter was no more peculiar than he was.

But there *was* something different about Peter, something that was much too complicated for Birdsall to comprehend. All Peter's life he had been confronted with choices: the 'normality' represented by his violent, womanizing father against the 'sissy' world of his adored but unvalued mother; the ruthlessly masculine versus the defencelessly feminine; the bully versus the victim. He learned early that men take what they want, sleep around, fight their way out of trouble; women are victims, dupes, lesser beings who exist for men's convenience. Being sensitive, kind, thoughtful, caring for other people, gets them nowhere. His mother had been all those things, even taking the young son of her husband's deaf and dumb girlfriend into her own house for a short period in 1976 when his mother's house was destroyed by fire, but she was broken in spirit by the time of her death in 1978. If Peter identified with his mother and hated his father, then he must be making a mistake, and such feelings were not only wrong but dangerous. Femininity was weak, fatal even. He certainly didn't want to end up like his mother. He would have to go out and *prove* that he was a man like his father, like his grandfather, like his brother Mick. Yet, when he'd tried his best to emulate them, he still didn't feel right. He didn't enjoy it as they did, the sex and the brawling and the bad language. In the end, his attempts to be a man just made things worse, brought home to him his failure, how *feminine* he was. There must be one final thing he hadn't tried, a way of eradicating this weakness within himself. And he found it only when he began ripping, stabbing, mutilating and *destroying* women's bodies.

This solution would not have been possible, had it not been for two elements in his background. One was his unusual familiarity with dead bodies, with decay and putrefaction, the legacy of his job in Bingley cemetery. Sutcliffe had long ago become accustomed to sights that would make other people puke; this was not a murderer who would be turned sick or who would panic at the sight of his own carnage. The other was his Catholic background. Although he was married in a Baptist chapel, Peter had been raised a docile and uncomplaining member of the Church. With his mother's milk he had imbibed its tenets: its obsession with death, its virulent antipathy to sex, its distaste for women. He learned that women fall into one of two groups, the madonnas and the whores. The whores are cunning temptresses, creatures tainted by sex, the daughters of Eve against whom men must be forever on their guard. This teaching accorded with his own experience, for were not his father and grandfather regular victims of the wiles of women who were no better than whores? And, as he grew older, he discovered he could go to certain streets any night of the week and see them offering their sordid wares. Not like his mother, that saintly woman who had, like the madonna, devoted her life to her children. Mothers to one side, whores to the other, that was clear enough. But then he started getting mixed up. His mother *wasn't* like the madonna, for wasn't she tainted by sex? First with his father—how else had he, Peter, come into being, not to mention his brothers and sisters?—and then with that man, the one she'd gone to meet in the pub on the terrible night his father caught her out. He began to fear, in his heart of hearts, that there weren't any madonnas, just whores.

No wonder he was relieved when he met Sonia, that inexperienced, childlike, curiously asexual being. She was different
in every way, from her slightly foreign accent to her strange,
arty, unprovocative clothes. For a time, the categories were restored, safely separate: he and Sonia would get married and
everything would be all right; whores in the outside world and
a madonna in his house. And life with Sonia, away from the
aggressively masculine Sutcliffes, would surely remove the pressure, the gnawing need to prove himself a man. The fantasy did
not last very long; two years into the courtship, five years before
their marriage, Sonia transgressed and the categories again broke
down. Sutcliffe discovered she'd been seeing another man, an
Italian who owned a sports car. The relationship was patched
up—perhaps because the fantasy was too important to Peter for
him to abandon it altogether—but his worst fear had been confirmed. There were no good women; some of them, like Sonia,
might look the part, but they were all the same underneath. So
he had his justification, ready made, when his fear of himself
became so great that it was no longer enough to deny the feminine, when he had not only to destroy but to see it destroyed.
That was what he meant when, much later, he told the police he
had wanted to kill prostitutes—not that he was seeking out
women who sold sex for a living, but that he knew all his victims
to be prostitutes simply because they were women. He had seen
the proof with his own eyes; no matter what they looked like
on top, no matter what they said or what they wore, they were
all the same underneath, their bodies gave them away. Each was
tainted by sex, by the lewd, flaunting breasts and round belly into
which he repeatedly plunged his screwdriver. He made no mis-
takes—how could he, there were none to be made—and the
glorious thing was that, now, suddenly, he was at peace with

himself. Until the doubts flooded back and he had to kill again.

At the beginning of 1981, everything went wrong. He was caught, put on trial, and sent to prison. There, in a closed world of men, the doubts swelled to a new peak. This time there was no release; his fragile self began to disintegrate. If the psychiatrists are correct, if Peter Sutcliffe is mad today, it is not necessarily because he was always so but because his safety valve has been taken away. Back in 1979, as the hunt for him became more desperate, football crowds in the north of England used to sing, to the tune of 'Guantanamera', 'There's only one Yorkshire Ripper'. They were both right and wrong. Peter Sutcliffe was always different, but not by a wide margin: the world is full of men who beat their wives, destroy their self-respect, treat them like dirt. They do it because they hate and despise women, because they are disgusted by them, because they need to prove to themselves and to their friends that they are real men. Occasionally, for one in a million, it isn't enough. Peter Sutcliffe was one of those. But when the trees are so dense, who can with certainty pick out the really rotten timber?

1 Ronald Gregory, *Mail on Sunday*, 26 June 1983.
2 *Sunday Mirror*, 4 November 1979.
3 A concise account of these events can be found in Susan Brownmiller, *Against Our Will*, Penguin, 1976, pp. 200–6 (Bantam, 1986). They are dealt with more fully in Gerold Frank, *The Boston Strangler*, Pan, 1967 (NAL, 1986).
4 Details of individual murders and attacks are drawn from numerous sources, including author's own interviews with survivors, newspaper and Press Association reports, the police summary of the case compiled in 1979, and Roger Cross, *The Yorkshire Ripper*, Granada, 1981.
5 Quoted in David Yallop, *Deliver Us From Evil*, Macdonald Futura, 1981, pp. 64–5.
6 Ibid., p. 66.
7 *Sunday Telegraph*, 23 November 1980.

8 Quoted in author's article, 'Getting Away With Murder', *New Socialist*, May/June 1982.

9 West Yorkshire Metropolitan Police, Special Notice: Murders And Assaults Upon Women In The North Of England, 13 September 1979.

10 John Sutcliffe's statement to police, read out at the Old Bailey by Sir Michael Havers, 5 May 1981.

11 *Mail on Sunday*, 26 June 1983.

12 *Evening News*, 26 October 1979.

13 *Sunday Times*, 8 November 1981.

14 *Sunday Times*, 23 November 1980.

15 *Yorkshire Post*, 9 March 1977.

16 Author's files.

17 Quoted in Donald Rumbelow, *The Complete Jack The Ripper*, W. H. Allen, 1987, p. 116 (Contemporary Books, 1988).

18 Ibid., pp. 116–24.

19 Author's files.

20 Author's article, 'Getting Away With Murder', *New Socialist*, as above.

21 *Mail on Sunday*, 3 July 1983.

22 Transcribed in police Special Notice, as above.

23 Evidence of John Leach, prison officer at Armley jail, Leeds, given at Old Bailey, 8 May 1981.

24 *Daily Express*, 14 April 1978.

25 *Yorkshire Evening Post*, 28 June 1977.

26 Evidence of Dr Malcolm MacCulloch at the Old Bailey, 15 May 1981.

27 Quoted in Cross, op. cit., p. 250, and the *Sun*, 23 May 1981; there is some disagreement as to whether Sutcliffe's lines were written out as prose or in the form of a poem.

28 *Sun*, 23 May 1981.

29 '. . . *Somebody's Husband, Somebody's Son*', Gordon Burn, Pan, 1985, p. 33 (Viking, 1985).

30 Ibid., p. 114.

31 Ibid., pp. 134–5.

32 *Evening Standard*, 5 January 1981.

33 Burn, op. cit., p. 161.

34 Cross, op. cit., p. 62.

35 *Sunday Mirror*, 24 May 1981.

36 *Daily Mirror*, 23 May 1981.

37 Cross, op. cit., p. 62.

38 Burn, op. cit., p. 146.

# POSTSCRIPT:
# BOYS WILL BE BOYS?

This is a book about lies—the lies men tell about women. It is about men who believe that women are dangerous, dishonest, provocative, and disgusting, that they must be controlled or they will do terrible damage to men. It is not about all men, just as it is not about all women. But the same themes come up again and again, whether they are expressed in the words of a second-century theologian, an F1-11 pilot, or an elderly peer in a gay novel. The beliefs and attitudes a judge takes into court when he tries a rape case are not far removed from those of the criminal in the dock, namely that a woman who oversteps certain narrowly drawn boundaries is asking for whatever she gets. It is about men who cannot cope with emotions, who blame women for their own feelings of sexual arousal, of inadequacy, of anger, for their terror of not being real men. It is also about the ways in which men attempt to justify the things they do to women, the violence and the discrimination, by pretending that the women are to blame, or that deep down it is what they want. And it is about the denial of female power, the manner in which women are imprisoned in male fantasies that allot them the status of eternal children, whether they happen to be the Princess of Wales, Marilyn Monroe, or the Virgin Mary. It is a book about connections, one whose aim is to establish through a process of 'insistence and repetition', to borrow a phrase from Roland Barthes, that misogyny is not the province of a few isolated individuals—not just of men, even, as I have shown in the chapters on Mrs Thatcher and Samantha Fox—but one of the concealed well-springs of our culture. It is a secret kept by men and women, because neither group wants to acknowledge what is really going on: men because they do not want to admit their fear of women's power, women because the truth is too uncomfortable to live with, and because they have been deceived. How often have women been told that their position is 'privileged', that they are 'the power behind the throne', or that they are the objects of special reverence? But for some women, the price of silence has become too great; this book is my contribution to the act of bringing the truth out into the open.

Where do we go from here? The natural reaction of anyone faced with this abundant mass of material is to ask why it is that men fear, hate and despise women. For me, that is to put the question the wrong way round. While we continue to organize ourselves as we do, how could men *not* hate women? Femininity is a strait-jacket, a ludicrous set of rules designed to keep women in their place, but it is certainly not hard to live up to. All a woman has to do is be passive, incompetent, helpless and whining—the last thing that is expected of the feminine woman is that she should actually achieve anything. Meanwhile men are driven by the need to succeed, to prove themselves, to be better than the next man, all without showing their feelings. Femininity enervates, masculinity warps.

There is a story about Denis, husband of Margaret Thatcher, which reveals a great deal about the flight from feeling triggered in conventional men by any situation that threatens to involve emotion. It refers to an incident when his and Margaret's children were still quite young, and the family had embarked on a car journey. Here it is in his own words, as reported in *The Spectator* (7 May 1988):

On the road to Portsmouth, it was . . . Carol and Mark
started bickering in the back. So I put my foot down. I
stopped the car and I said: 'Right, you three—get out.'
So they got out of the car. And I said: 'Right, Margaret!
Deal with 'em.'

The phrase 'I put my foot down' is misleading; rather than
taking control of the situation, Denis's reaction is to abandon it
to his wife. His irritation over the incident clearly extends to her
('Right, you *three*'), it being her job to ensure that the head of
the family is not troubled by scenes of this nature. He even orders
them out of the car, ejecting them and their messy feelings from
his space. It is a perfect piece of masculine behaviour, an inability
to cope which finds its solution in transferring the problem—and
the emotion it has stirred up—to a woman.

Some people's response—the majority response, I suspect—
to this story would be to argue that Denis Thatcher's behaviour
was old-fashioned, a bit heavy-handed, perhaps, but essentially
*natural*. At the very beginning of this book, in the introduction,
I referred briefly to the anatomy-is-destiny theory of difference
between the sexes and said that I did not believe it. Throughout
this book I have tried to show that masculine behaviour and
feminine behaviour, far from being natural, are the means of
enforcing an *unnatural* separation between men and women in
order to maintain an unstable and unjust power structure. The
result is a state of covert warfare between the sexes in which,
while not all men are rapists, every woman is a potential victim.

I do not pretend to have easy answers to the questions raised
by this book; my intention is to open a discussion, not to close
it. Nor do I claim superior knowledge of the channels through
which misogyny has invaded our culture, or the means of revers-
ing its flow; I have simply tried to chart its course. But it seems

to me undeniable that our search for the origin of the woman-hating which poisons our relationships must begin with the forced march of the sexes into two opposed camps. The process starts at birth, and it is one of the chief paradoxes of our culture that the welfare of its children, its *future*, is placed almost exclusively in the hands of people of low status, a class it holds in contempt. It would be foolish to claim that this is a complete explanation of how we come to find ourselves in a situation of such sheer awfulness, or that minor adjustments to our methods of child-rearing could wipe out misogyny overnight. But it is a starting-point. And the fact that some men have already recognized the lethal nature of the attitudes they absorbed as they grew up is an optimistic sign of the possibility of change. They have recognized masculinity for what it is, a means of denying equal status to women, a construct whose purpose is the maintenance of a power structure based on men's superior physical strength and which long ago became redundant. Misogyny is its inevitable by-product; we teach men that women are inferior from the cradle, and they spend their lives struggling, against the evidence, to convince themselves that this is the case. Men are the victims of lies, just as much as women. It is only when we dare to confront this reality together that we will have reason to hope for the future.

Thanks are due to the following for permission to reprint extracts from the titles listed.

Angus and Robertson (UK) for *Charles and Diana: Inside a Royal Marriage* by Judy Wade (1987); Bantam Doubleday Dell for *Royal Wedding* by Mary Christopher (1982); Basil Blackwell Ltd for *Male Fantasies* by Klaus Theweleit (1987); Bloomsbury for *Presumed Innocent* by Scott Turow (1987); Bodley Head-Jonathan Cape Ltd and Random House, Inc. for *Sophie's Choice* by William Styron. Copyright © 1976, 1978, 1979 by William Styron. David Bolt Associates for *Order of Assassins: The Psychology of Murder* by Colin Wilson (1975); Bunch Publishers Ltd for 'Daily Girls No 5'; Cambridge University Press for *Catullus and his World* by T. P. Wiseman (1985); Capital Newspapers (*Hackney Gazette*) (1986); Chatto and Windus for 'The Ballad of the Yorkshire Ripper' by Blake Morrison and *The Swimming-Pool Library* by Alan Hollinghurst (1988); Christ Church College, Oxford, and Edward Mendelson for 'Ode to the New Year' by W. H. Auden (1939); T & T Clark Ltd for 'On Female Dress' (De Cultu Feminarum), Tertullian, Writings, Vol 1, from the Ante-Nicene Christian Library Series (1869); Curtis Brown Ltd for *Poets in a Landscape* by Gilbert Highet. Copyright © 1957 by Gilbert Highet, and for *Princess* text © by Robert Lacey (1982); *Daily Express* (1978); *Daily Mirror* (1981); *Daily Telegraph* (1986, 1987 and 1988); *Evening News* (1979); *Evening Standard* (1981); extracts from the Authorized King James Version of the Bible, the rights of which are vested in the Crown in perpetuity within the United Kingdom, are reproduced by permission of Eyre and Spottiswoode Publishers, Her Majesty's Printers, London; Gollancz (Victor) Ltd for *Deliver Us From Evil* (1981); Grafton Books for *The Yorkshire Ripper* by Roger Cross (1981); *Guardian* (1988); Hamish Hamilton Ltd for *Sixty-Eight: The Year of the Barricades* by David Caute (1988); William Heinemann Ltd for *Somebody's Husband, Somebody's Son* by Gordon Burn (1985); Heron Enterprises Ltd for *Arabella* by Georgette Heyer (1949); David Higham Associates Ltd for *Christopher Isherwood: A Personal Memoir* by John Lehmann (1987); *Indepen-*

*dent* (1987 and 1988); Johns Hopkins University Press for *Pandora's Daughters: The Role and Status of Women in Greek and Roman Antiquity* by Eva Cantarella (1987); Michael Joseph for *The Ultimate Family: The Making of the Royal House of Windsor* by John Pearson (1987) and for *If This is a Man* and *The Truce* by Primo Levi (1987); Alfred A. Knopf Inc. for *Forbidden Colours* by Yukio Mishima (1971); *London Standard* for 'Epitaph for Christobel' by Maureen Cleave (1986); *Mail on Sunday* (1983 and 1988); James Michie for *The Poems of Catullus* (1972); *New Socialist* for 'Getting Away with Murder' by Joan Smith (1982); *News of the World* (1987 and 1988); W. W. Norton & Co for 'The Dread of Women' from *Feminine Psychology* by Karen Horney (1967); Paladin for *The Female Eunuch* by Germaine Greer (1970); Paulist Press for 'An Exhortation to Chastity' (De Exhortatione Castitatis) trans. in Tertullian, *Treatises on Marriage and Remarriage* by William P. Le Saint (1951); Penguin Books Ltd for *Juvenal: The Sixteen Satires* trans. by Peter Green copyright © Peter Green (1967 and 1974) and for *The Romans* by R. H. Barrow, copyright © R. H. Barrow (1949) and for *Plato: The Symposium* trans. by Walter Hamilton (1951) and for *Eton Voices* by Danny Danzinger (1988) and for *Rolle: The Fire of Love* trans. by Clifton Wolters (Penguin Classics, 1972), copyright © Clifton Wolters (1971); Putnam Publishing Group for *Marilyn: A Biography* by Norman Mailer (1979); Secker and Warburg Ltd for *Forbidden Colours* by Yukio Mishima (1968); Anthony Sheil Associates Ltd for *Thatcher* by Nicholas Wapshott and George Brock (1983); The Society of Authors on behalf of the Estate of Compton Mackenzie for *Thin Ice* (1956); Stein and Day Publishers for *My Story* copyright © 1974 by Marilyn Monroe; *Sunday Times* (1982); A. P. Watt Ltd on behalf of Michael B. Yeats and Macmillan London Ltd for 'The Scholars' taken from *The Collected Poems of W. B. Yeats* (1961); Viking Penguin, a division of Penguin Books USA Inc., for *Somebody's Husband, Somebody's Son* by Gordon Burn copyright © 1984 by Gordon Burn; Virago Press for *The Sadeian Woman* by Angela Carter (1979) and for 'The White Brothel: The Literary Exoneration of the Pornographic' by Susanne Kappeler from *Sexuality, A Reader*, edited by *Feminist Review* (1987).